T0323983

# Cambridge Elements ≣

Elements in the Philosophy of Mathematics
edited by
Penelope Rush
*University of Tasmania*
Stewart Shapiro
*The Ohio State University*

# ELEMENTS OF PURITY

## Andrew Arana
*University of Lorraine*

CAMBRIDGE
UNIVERSITY PRESS

Shaftesbury Road, Cambridge CB2 8EA, United Kingdom

One Liberty Plaza, 20th Floor, New York, NY 10006, USA

477 Williamstown Road, Port Melbourne, VIC 3207, Australia

314–321, 3rd Floor, Plot 3, Splendor Forum, Jasola District Centre, New Delhi – 110025, India

103 Penang Road, #05–06/07, Visioncrest Commercial, Singapore 238467

Cambridge University Press is part of Cambridge University Press & Assessment, a department of the University of Cambridge.

We share the University's mission to contribute to society through the pursuit of education, learning and research at the highest international levels of excellence.

www.cambridge.org
Information on this title: www.cambridge.org/9781009539708

DOI: 10.1017/9781009052719

When citing this work, please include a reference to the DOI 10.1017/9781009052719

First published 2024

*A catalogue record for this publication is available from the British Library*

ISBN 978-1-009-53970-8 Hardback
ISBN 978-1-009-05589-5 Paperback
ISSN 2399-2883 (online)
ISSN 2514-3808 (print)

# Elements of Purity

Elements in the Philosophy of Mathematics

DOI: 10.1017/9781009052719
First published online: November 2024

Andrew Arana
*University of Lorraine*

**Author for correspondence:** Andrew Arana, andrew.arana@univ-lorraine.fr

**Abstract:** A proof of a theorem can be said to be pure if it draws only on what is "close" or "intrinsic" to that theorem. In this Element we will investigate the apparent preference for pure proofs that has persisted in mathematics since antiquity, alongside a competing preference for impurity. In Section 1, we present two examples of purity, from geometry and number theory. In Section 2, we give a brief history of purity in mathematics. In Section 3, we discuss several different types of purity, based on different measures of distance between theorem and proof. In Section 4 we discuss reasons for preferring pure proofs, for the varieties of purity constraints presented in Section 3. In Section 5 we conclude by reflecting briefly on purity as a preference for the local and how issues of translation intersect with the considerations we have raised throughout this work.

**Keywords:** purity, mathematical practice, philosophy of mathematics, epistemology of mathematics, normativity of mathematics

ISBNs: 9781009539708 (HB), 9781009055895 (PB), 9781009052719 (OC)
ISSNs: 2399-2883 (online), 2514-3808 (print)

# Contents

# 1 Purity in Practice

Roughly, a proof of a theorem is *pure* if it draws only on what is "close" or "intrinsic" to that theorem. Other language commonly found in the mathematical literature says that a proof is pure if it avoids what is "extrinsic," "extraneous," "distant," "remote," "alien," or "foreign" to what is being proved. The best way to start with understanding purity in mathematics is to see it in practice. In this section we will present a case study from geometry, on the classical theorem of Menelaus from planar Euclidean geometry as studied by Einstein, and a second one from number theory, on Jacobi's four squares theorem.

## 1.1 Einstein on Purity in Geometry

We begin with a case study discussed by Luchins and Luchins (1990), from which we take the translations in this section. In 1937 Albert Einstein corresponded with his friend Max Wertheimer, the Gestalt psychologist, about "the problem of axioms." Seeking to understand Wertheimer's problem better, Einstein asked if Wertheimer wanted "to compare the value of two proofs which are *themselves based* on the same system of (concepts and) axioms." He added that "in that case, surely, we are completely satisfied only if we feel of each intermediate concept that it has to do with the proposition to be proved."

To clarify this, Einstein then presents two proofs of the theorem of Menelaus as "a pretty example of two proofs of different degrees of perspicuity." The theorem of Menelaus says that if $\triangle ABC$ is a triangle, and $\ell$ is a line that crosses the sides $BC$, $CA$, $AB$ at three distinct points $P$, $Q$, $R$, then

$$\frac{AR}{RB} \cdot \frac{BP}{PC} \cdot \frac{CQ}{QA} = 1.$$

Figure 1 shows the basic configuration of the theorem.

Einstein then gives two proofs of Menelaus, one of which he calls "ugly", the other "elegant". The first proof brings in additional, seemingly unrelated constructions, while the second proof restricts itself to what is mentioned in Meneleus' theorem.

The "ugly" proof relies on what he calls the "principle of similarity", otherwise known as the theorem of Thales (Euclid VI.2; see Figure 2). It says: let $\triangle ABC$ be a triangle and let $DE$ be parallel to $BC$, cutting the other two sides at $D$ and $E$. Then $\frac{AD}{DB} = \frac{AE}{EC}$.

The "ugly" proof then goes as follows. Augment the Menelaus configuration by a line $OA$ parallel to the transversal $PR$ (see Figure 3). By one application

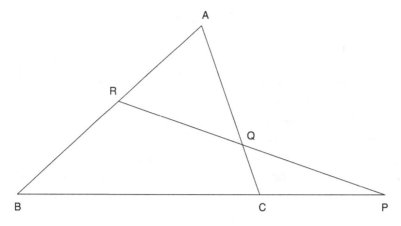

**Figure 1** Theorem of Menelaus.

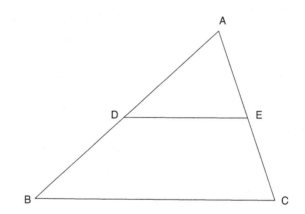

**Figure 2** Theorem of Thales.

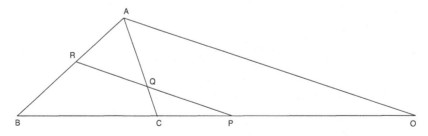

**Figure 3** "Ugly" proof of Menelaus.

of Thales, we get that $\frac{CQ}{QA} = \frac{PC}{PO}$. By a second application of Thales, we get that $\frac{RB}{AR} = \frac{BP}{PO}$. We have that

$$\frac{CQ}{QA} = \frac{PC}{PO} \text{ and } \frac{RB}{AR} = \frac{BP}{PO}.$$

Solving both for *PO* and then setting both equal, we have

$$\frac{QA \cdot PC}{CQ} = \frac{AR \cdot BP}{RB}.$$

Rearranging terms, we get

$$\frac{AR}{RB} \cdot \frac{BP}{PC} \cdot \frac{CQ}{QA} = 1.$$

This is the theorem of Menelaus.

For the "elegant proof," Einstein uses the "principle that two triangles with a common (or supplementary) angle are related as the products of the adjacent sides," and writes it in an equation involving a proportion of the triangles themselves and the adjacent sides. See again Figure 1. For the triangles $\triangle ARQ$ and $\triangle BRP$, Einstein uses this principle to get

$$\frac{\triangle ARQ}{\triangle BRP} = \frac{AR \cdot QR}{BR \cdot RP}.$$

But what is an equation involving a triangle? A triangle is not a quantity. If we read the "principle" as involving the *areas* of triangles, however, then it can be understood as an application of the trigonometric formula for the area of a triangle. This formula says that for a triangle $\triangle ABC$ with angle $\angle ABC = \theta$, we have that

$$area(\triangle ABC) = \frac{1}{2} \cdot AB \cdot BC \sin \theta.$$

For $\triangle ABC$ and $\triangle DEF$ with a common angle $\angle ABC = \angle DEF = \theta$, we then have

$$\frac{area(\triangle ABC)}{area(\triangle DEF)} = \frac{\frac{1}{2} \cdot AB \cdot BC \sin \theta}{\frac{1}{2} \cdot DE \cdot EF \sin \theta} = \frac{AB \cdot BC}{DE \cdot EF}.$$

If $\angle ABC$ and $\angle DEF$ are supplementary, then $\sin(\angle ABC) = \sin(\angle DEF)$.

The "elegant proof" applies the formula

$$\frac{area(\triangle ABC)}{area(\triangle DEF)} = \frac{AB \cdot BC}{DE \cdot EF}$$

three times, on the triangles formed by the vertices of the given triangle with the corresponding segments of the transversal. It then multiplies the resulting equations together, giving the conclusion of Menelaus.

First, apply the formula to $\triangle ARQ$ and $\triangle BRP$, where $\angle ARQ$ and $\angle BRP$ are supplementary, obtaining

$$\frac{area(\triangle ARQ)}{area(\triangle BRP)} = \frac{AR \cdot QR}{RB \cdot PR}.$$

Next, apply the formula to $\triangle BRP$ and $\triangle QPC$, with common angle $\angle QPC$, obtaining

$$\frac{area(\triangle BRP)}{area(\triangle QPC)} = \frac{PR \cdot BP}{QP \cdot PC}.$$

Finally, apply the formula to $\triangle QPC$ and $\triangle ARQ$, with common = opposite angle $\angle AQR$, obtaining

$$\frac{area(\triangle QPC)}{area(\triangle ARQ)} = \frac{QP \cdot CQ}{QA \cdot QR}.$$

We then have

$$\frac{area(\triangle ARQ)}{area(\triangle BRP)} = \frac{AR \cdot QR}{RB \cdot PR},$$

$$\frac{area(\triangle BRP)}{area(\triangle QPC)} = \frac{PR \cdot BP}{QP \cdot PC},$$

$$\frac{area(\triangle QPC)}{area(\triangle ARQ)} = \frac{QP \cdot CQ}{QA \cdot QR}.$$

Now multiply both sides of these three equations together. The left-hand side reduces to 1 because in the three terms being multiplied, the area of the three triangles occurs once in a numerator and once in a denominator. We thus obtain

$$1 = \frac{AR \cdot QR}{RB \cdot PR} \cdot \frac{PR \cdot BP}{QP \cdot PC} \cdot \frac{QP \cdot CQ}{QA \cdot QR}$$

$$= \frac{AR \cdot \cancel{QR}}{RB \cdot \cancel{PR}} \cdot \frac{\cancel{PR} \cdot BP}{\cancel{QP} \cdot PC} \cdot \frac{\cancel{QP} \cdot CQ}{QA \cdot \cancel{QR}}$$

$$= \frac{AR}{RB} \cdot \frac{BP}{PC} \cdot \frac{CQ}{QA},$$

cancelling the segments $QR$, $PR$, $QP$ of the transversal that appear in both numerators and denominators of the expressions. We have thus obtained the conclusion of Menelaus.

Why does Einstein call the first proof "ugly" and the second proof "elegant"? Einstein replies: "Although the first proof is somewhat simpler, it is not satisfying. For it uses an auxiliary line which has nothing to do with the content of the proposition to be proved." By contrast, "the second proof … can be read off directly from the figure."

The thought is that the auxiliary line in the first proof is unrelated to the "content" of the theorem of Menelaus, and this renders it ugly. He clarifies this in his comment about the second proof, saying that it can be "read off directly" from the triangle given in the theorem of Menelaus. Every element of the second proof is part of the given triangle and thus contains nothing extraneous to the content of the theorem. The first proof augments the Menelaus configuration by a line parallel to the given transversal, whereas the second adds nothing to the configuration. Einstein judges that this use of an additional element, not part of the original configuration, is to be avoided if we seek "'elegant" proofs. He thus deems his second proof "better" because it avoids what is extraneous to what is being proved, and is more elegant because of its relative minimality.

Einstein's remarks are the occasion to introduce the central concern of this Element, *purity of methods*. Roughly, a proof of a theorem, or a solution to a problem, is *pure* if it draws only on what is "close" or "intrinsic" to that theorem or problem. Since this rough reckoning of purity invokes a notion of distance, purity can come in degrees; and if a threshold is set, proofs involving what is more remote than that threshold can be said to be impure *tout court*. In Einstein's case, the distance between proof and theorem is measured by what belongs to the "content" of the theorem of Menelaus, and the purer proof is better because it is more elegant than the less pure proof. These remarks frame two focal questions for investigating purity constraints. Firstly, how is purity to be measured? Secondly, why is purity, measured this way, valuable? As we will see, purity constraints of many different kinds arise in mathematical practice. For each such constraint, the nature of its measure of purity should be determined, and the reasons for preferring such proofs should be examined.

Let us look more closely at the first question in Einstein's case. In a follow-up letter to Wertheimer, Einstein seeks to specify his measure of purity more fully. He expresses discomfort even with the second, "better" proof. "A certain uneasiness remains, however, even in the better proof," he writes, "since we don't see a priori what the *segments* on the transversal are supposed to have to do with the matter. We use them in the proof, and then they are cancelled out." These segments of the transversal aren't mentioned in the theorem (even though the transversal itself is). Moreover, though they are used in the proof, they cancel each other out during a calculation, furthering the sense that they are unnecessarily brought into the proof. Einstein may be suggesting that since the segments on the transversal are not *explicitly* mentioned in the statement of Menelaus, they are not permissible in a pure proof of it. While until now the notion of content used in his purity has remained vague, here Einstein moves away from a potential semantic understanding of it toward a syntactic understanding. On this measure, only what is *explicitly* mentioned in a statement can be used in a pure proof.

Many other proofs of the theorem of Menelaus are known (compare Chemla 1998), and many fail Einstein's purity constraint. For instance, we can add auxiliary perpendiculars to the original configuration and apply principles of similarity to arrive at the conclusion. We can also use coordinate methods as in Cartesian geometry. Both of these methods go beyond the content of the theorem in Einstein's sense, as neither these perpendiculars nor coordinates are part of the formulation of Menelaus as considered here.

## 1.2 Purity in Number Theory: Jacobi's Four Squares Theorem

At the end of the nineteenth century, Friedrich Engel (1890) published a short book on taste in mathematics. Engel is today best known as the coauthor with Sophus Lie of the monumental three-volume *Theorie der Transformations-gruppen* (1888, 1890, 1893), which gave a detailed introduction and treatment of what would soon be known as Lie groups. But Engel was also an astute commentator on mathematics, as Engel (1890) reveals. Near the end, Engel considers the state of number theory at the end of the nineteenth century:

> Number theory deals with the properties of integers, so one should actually demand that it prove all of its theorems without leaving the realm of integers. But there is still a long way to go before she can do that. A good number of apparently extremely simple theorems have hitherto only been able to be proved with the use of an enormous apparatus of transcendent means, of theorems from the theory of elliptic functions, and the like. (p. 20)

Engel here describes the status of purity in number theory, pointing to elementary arithmetic theorems proved by transcendental means. In this section we will describe one such theorem, though as we will see, it is not one that eluded purely arithmetic proof. The case, Jacobi's four squares theorem, will rather show how this impurity came to be brought to a celebrated result of number theory and how the actors involved in this case thought of it.

In 1621 Claude Gaspar Bachet de Méziriac published a Latin edition of Diophantus' *Arithmetic*, in which, in addition to his translation, Bachet added his own commentaries. In Book IV, Problem 31, he comments that every positive integer can be written as the sum of four squares, verifying the result explicitly up to 120 and saying that he verified it up to 325. He adds that it "can easily be extended to any number of squares" (compare Diophantus 1621, p. 242).

Bachet's conjecture almost immediately captured the imagination of mathematicians. Fermat (1894) agreed with Bachet that Diophantus had known the theorem, writing in a letter to Mersenne in 1636 that Bachet had verified it experimentally but had no proof (pp. 65–66). In 1638 Descartes (1898) too wrote of the conjecture to Mersenne, saying that it was "doubtlessly one of the most beautiful that one could find concerning numbers" but that he knew no proof and that he judged it so difficult that he did not dare to start looking for one (p. 256). Fermat learned of Descartes' remarks and seems to have taken that as further motivation to solve it himself. Noting Descartes' difficulties with the problem in a letter to Carcavi in 1659, Fermat (1894), claims to have found a proof by his method of infinite descent, but does not give the proof (p. 433). (Incidentally, it was in a copy of Bachet's edition of Diophantus that Fermat wrote his infamous marginal comment on what would become known as his Last Theorem.) Euler then worked on the problem but it was only in 1770 that Lagrange, building on Euler's work, published the first proof (see Lagrange 1772).

After seeing that every positive integer can be written as the sum of four squares, we can ask in how many different ways it can be done. For instance, Bachet observed that 39 can be written as $1 + 1 + 1 + 36 = 1^2 + 1^2 + 1^2 + 6^2$ and as $1+4+9+25 = 1^2+2^2+3^2+5^2$. Are there any other combinations that work? Jacobi (1829) turned to this question and solved it (p. 106). The result he proved is now known as *Jacobi's four squares theorem*: the number of representations of $n$ as a sum of four squares is 8 times the sum of the positive divisors of $n$ that are not divisible by 4. It follows that 39 can be represented in $8 \cdot 56 = 448$ ways, since the positive divisors of 39 are $1, 3, 13, 39$ and their sum is 56.

To see a little more clearly how this works, let's consider a simpler example, 8. The positive divisors of 8 are $1, 2, 4$, and 8, and of these, 1 and 2 are not divisible by 4. Jacobi's four squares theorem says that 8 is representable in $(1 + 2) \cdot 8 = 24$ ways as the sum of four squares. Trivially 0 is a square, and 4 is a square in two ways, as $2^2$ and as $(-2)^2$. So, 8 can be written as the sum of four squares in the following four ways: $0 + 0 + 2^2 + 2^2, 0 + 0 + (-2)^2 + (-2)^2,$ $0+0+2^2+(-2)^2, 0+0+(-2)^2+2^2$. Order matters here, so these cases need to be distinguished. Similarly, there are six total places where the 4s can go: the last two places as we have seen, the second and fourth places, and so on. Since for each of these placements of the 4s there are four ways that the numbers can be summed, as we saw earlier, we obtain 6 times 4 equals 24 ways, as Jacobi's result says.

While this purely arithmetic result is simple to state, the proof that Jacobi (1829) presents in *Fundamenta nova theoriae functionum ellipticarum* uses, as the name indicates, the theory of elliptic functions. Elliptic functions in Jacobi's hands were obtained by inverting elliptic integrals, which were introduced in attempts to find the arc lengths of ellipses. In this development, elliptic functions were thought of as functions of complex variables, though Jacobi's treatment of complex variables in this work was purely formal rather than a development of complex analysis (compare Gray 2015, pp. 88–89). Nevertheless, Jacobi's proof of his four squares theorem was breathtakingly transcendental. He defines an elliptic function known today as a theta function, a function of a complex variable, and shows that it is periodic. As this is a periodic function, he can then find a Fourier series representing this function. From this series he can read off a power series whose coefficients, following the work of Euler, have a combinatorial interpretation: they give the number of ways a positive integer can be represented as the sum of four squares (compare Hardy and Wright 1979, chapters 19 and 20).

In so doing, Jacobi brings methods that seem to be quite remote from elementary arithmetic to bear on a simply stated arithmetic theorem. In his announcement of the theorem in Jacobi (1828), he writes that this result "seems to be difficult to prove by the known methods of number theory" and that his proof "by the theory of elliptic functions is entirely analytic" (p. 191). He lauded his proof as having bridged two domains previously thought distant. In Jacobi (1848), he wrote: "Between analysis and number theory, which were long thought to be completely separate disciplines, more and more frequent and often unexpected connections and transitions have recently been discovered. A rich source of mutual relationships between the two, which will remain unexhausted for a long time, is the analysis of elliptic functions" (p. 61). He saw his work on the four squares theorem in this light.

At the same time, he recognized that not everyone would be satisfied with an analytic proof of this elementary result. In Jacobi (1834), he observes:

> This theorem is clear even at first glance by comparing the formulas that I have shown in *Fundamenta nova theoriae functionum ellipticarum*. But for the sake of the men of arithmetic, not advocating analytic developments, I will show the matter here, in place of the above-mentioned propositions, starting solely from the theorems that concern the composition of numbers into two squares. You can extract such a demonstration without much trouble from the analysis that we have used on page 109. The less it is concealed, the more likely it can provide a handle for others to further refine the method that I use in what follows. (p. 167)

If he is not himself troubled by the distance between the theorem and the proof, he acknowledges that others might be, the "*virorum arithmeticorum*," and accordingly gives a new, purely arithmetic proof. This new proof applies a result about the representation of positive integers by two squares that was known to Fermat and proved by Euler by purely arithmetic means (see Euler 1758). Moreover, Jacobi observes that his new proof was "concealed" by the analysis, but can be revealed without difficulty, and that this revelation might help mathematicians skilled in arithmetic make further progress on purely arithmetic problems.

Jacobi continued to apply his transcendental methods to number-theoretic problems and also continued to try to translate these proofs into purely arithmetic terms. He commented on these parallel aims again in Jacobi (1848). Firstly, he argued for the value of his transcendental proofs:

> The derivation of these arithmetic propositions from the analytic developments not only increases the supply of arithmetic proofs, but also the propositions themselves are found in a new, remarkable form. In an earlier case, in which a fundamentally arithmetic theorem resulted as the corollary of an elliptic formula, this theorem received an essentially different version, which gave it a more general character and increased importance. (p. 65)

By grounding an arithmetic result in a transcendental context, the result gains in generality, as it is now seen to be part of a wider conceptual network. Again, such impurity is not necessary, since purely arithmetic proofs are also available by "translating" the transcendental proof into arithmetic terms:

> In the following I have tried to derive the properties of the numbers resulting from analytic developments also from well-known arithmetic theorems, which every time gives a purely arithmetic proof for the analytic formula. Although these arithmetic proofs of results obtained by analytical means do not present any essential difficulties, they are sometimes of a complicated nature. (p. 67)

Thus, while purely arithmetic proofs can be found without difficulty, they can be more complex than the transcendental proofs, though Jacobi does not specify what kind of complexity he has in mind.

Jacobi thus reveals a certain ambivalence about the apparent impurity of his transcendental proof: on the one hand, it bridges what were earlier thought to be distinct branches of mathematics and is valuable for doing so; on the other hand, this "bridge" can be translated into purely arithmetic terms without too much difficulty, using the aforementioned combinatorial interpretations of power series by Euler. However, these translations can be more complex than the original impure proofs; but still, the pure proofs can be useful in helping experts in arithmetic advance their arithmetic studies.

Mathematicians after Jacobi continued to refine his new methods. Eisenstein, who was involved in a controversy with Jacobi over their proofs of certain reciprocity laws (see Collison 1977), found another purely arithmetic proof of Jacobi's four squares theorem, but judged his results to not be mere translations of transcendental methods: "In my investigations these propositions are proved by purely arithmetic considerations, and appear as special cases of more general propositions" (see Eisenstein 1847, p. 135). For similar reasons Dirichlet too sought a new purely arithmetic proof of Jacobi's theorem. In 1856 an extract of a letter from Dirichlet to Liouville was published (Dirichlet 1856) in which Dirichlet recalls a recent conversation they had had about Jacobi's "beau" theorem. He observes that Jacobi "first proved by his elliptic series and has since given an arithmetic demonstration ... [but] which Jacobi himself warned was only a translation of the first proof" (p. 210). Dirichlet says he has already looked for a long time for other principles on which to found the theorem, but that is not the subject of his letter today. Instead, it is to simplify Jacobi's purely arithmetic proof by "exposing the arithmetic or rather algebraic fact that forms its principal foundation." While there may exist straightforward ways to render the transcendental methods arithmetic, the pure proof resulting from this translation is not particularly clear. Here he echoes Jacobi himself. There is reason, says Dirichlet, to search for new proofs that are more clearly situated within arithmetic, rather than awkwardly replicating the analytic structure in arithmetic language.

## 1.3  Summing up the Case Studies

In these two case studies two type of purity seem to be involved. Einstein looks for a proof that does not draw on resources beyond what is needed to determine the content of the theorem he is proving. Jacobi, by contrast, looks for a proof that stays within the domain or branch of the theorem he is proving. We will go on to call the former type of purity "topical" and the latter, "geographical." We will come to distinguish other types of purity as well, and discuss how these types of purity are related.

## 1.4  Purity of Proof vs. Purity of Definition

In this Element we will focus on treating purity of *proof*. But purity concerns arise for other mathematical practices as well, such as *definition*. For instance, Samuel Eilenberg and Norman Samuel Eilenberg and Norman Steenrod (1945) sought an axiomatic definition of the concept of homology group in algebraic topology, invoking purity as a constraint on their search:

> The usual approach to homology theory is by way of the somewhat compli-
> cated idea of a complex. In order to arrive at a purely topological concept, the
> student of the subject is required to wade patiently through a large amount of
> analytic geometry. Many of the ideas used in the constructions, such as ori-
> entation, chain and algebraic boundary, seem artificial. The motivation for
> their use appears only in retrospect. (p. 117)

The purely algebraico-topological concept of homology group should not be defined using analytic geometry, they write, alluding to its development by Henri Poincaré with its attachment to particular topological spaces. Never-theless, their interest in a topologically pure definition of homology group was linked to their interest in topologically pure proofs. In their textbook (Eilenberg & Steenrod 1952, p. x), they add that "Proofs based directly on the axioms are usually simple and conceptual. It is no longer necessary for a proof to be burdened with the heavy machinery used to define the homology groups." Their pure definition of homology group thus leads to topologically pure proofs. The quest for "good" definitions in mathematics is frequently linked to the values realized by proofs from such definitions (see Tappenden 2008), and so we will continue to focus principally on purity of proof.

## 1.5 Looking Ahead

In this Element we will investigate the apparent preference for pure proofs that has persisted in mathematics since antiquity, alongside a competing preference for impurity. In Section 2, we'll give a brief history of purity in mathematics. We'll then, in Section 3, discuss several different types of purity, based on several different measures of distance between theorem and proof. In Section 4 we'll discuss reasons for preferring pure proofs, for the varieties of purity constraints presented in Section 3. In Section 5 we conclude by reflecting briefly on purity as a preference for the local and how issues of translation intersect with the considerations we have raised throughout this Element.

## 2 A Brief History of Purity

In his biographical notice for Kurt Gödel, Georg Kreisel (1980) wrote about Hilbert's interest in purity, putting it in historical context in the following way:

> Hilbert was quite conscious of … an age-old ideal of *Methodenreinheit*, as he stressed in the peroration to Hilbert (1899); 'age-old' in that it goes back to the time of the Greeks when Archimedes was criticized for using properties of space to prove theorems about the plane; cf. Knorr (1978). For elementary theorems, you use elementary cuts. Number theorists will think of heated but inarticulate arguments about impure methods, analytic number theory at one time, 1-adic cohomology now. Incidentally, though this was not stressed by Hilbert himself, his later, much more famous consistency programme is also a particular case of this search for pure methods: so-called finitist theorems should have finitist proofs (of which old-fashioned school mathematics is typical). (p. 163)

As Kreisel indicates, the search for purity and its counterideal, impurity, has been a part of mathematical practice since antiquity. Despite the profound changes in mathematical practice and in philosophical conceptions of it since then, it remains so today. In this section we will come to see better why this is.

Thinking about purity requires that we attend to what Jean-Michel Salanskis has called the "geographicity" of mathematics: that mathematics is divided into branches and has always been (cf. Salanskis 2008). As Salanskis observes, the "map" of mathematics is as unstable and relative as are maps of Europe or the world across the centuries. Given that at any time mathematics is divided into branches in one way or another, each branch can be expected to develop its own local practices and norms. This kind of "internal regionalization" as Salanskis puts it, or "localism" as we prefer to put it, is a feature of debates about purity over time.

This concern had a central place in Aristotle's theory of knowledge. In the *Posterior Analytics*, he says that

> Understanding must be knowledge of a necessary nexus, and therefore must clearly be obtained through a necessary middle term; otherwise its possessor will know neither the cause nor the fact that his conclusion is a necessary connexion.... It follows that we cannot, in demonstrating, pass from one genus to another. We cannot, for instance, prove geometrical truths by arithmetic.

Reasoning which crossed generic lines in this way was termed *metabasis* and could not provide for understanding. Such demonstrations could provide knowledge, but not of the best kind that he called scientific (epistēmē). Purity for Aristotle was thus an *ideal of proof*. The value of pure proofs, Aristotle indicates, is rooted in their revelation of a necessary connection between the subject and predicate of the theorem proved. Since a premiss of an Aristotelian demonstration is supposed to express the essence of the subject concerned, as Michael Detlefsen (2008) explains:

> A pure proof provided knowledge that the predicate of its conclusion (the minor term of the proof) held of its subject (the major term) solely because of *what* the subject in itself was. It showed the very *whatness* (i.e. the essence) of the subject of a theorem to be the 'cause' of its having the property expressed by its predicate. (p. 180)

Aristotle's theory of knowledge thus supported the idea that individual mathematical disciplines were autonomous, with their own distinct first principles (see Steinkrüger 2018).

Ancient mathematicians had a keen awareness of the geographicity of mathematics, reflected in Aristotle's mathematical example of kind-crossing. They were also attentive to other aspects of the organization of mathematics that gave rise to different understandings of purity. Proclus (1992) attends to one such understanding in his commentary on book I of the *Elements*. He notes Euclid's attention to what is more "elementary" in geometry and observes that the *Elements* is organized by the search for proofs of less elementary propositions by more elementary ones. In so doing, results are established with clarity and generality (p. 61). This type of purity is, on the face of it, rather different from the "topical" purity of Aristotle, concerned with mathematical genera. Proclus talks instead of an elemental purity, in which a proposition should be proved using only what is no less elementary than that proposition. For instance, Proclus remarks on the efforts in antiquity to prove the parallel postulate rather than take it as a hypothesis, because of its lack of self-evidence relative to the other postulates. He then shows how Book I of the *Elements* is organized in three parts: a first part on triangles, a second part on parallelograms, and a third part demonstrating the "kinship" of triangles and parallelograms by showing they have similar properties to each other and, finally, by relating the two in the Pythagorean theorem (*Ibid.*, pp. 68–69). This organization induces preferences for certain proofs over others; for instance, Proclus lauds Euclid's proof of Proposition 21, about triangles, for not using parallel lines, suggesting that others at the time used parallels (*Ibid.*, p. 256). In avoiding the less-elementary notion of parallel line in favor of the notions and methods already treated in Book I at that point, Euclid's proof of I.21 is elementally pure.

The development of algebra at the birth of the modern era would bring a shock to the Aristotelian model of knowledge and thus of purity (see Klein 1992, Rabouin 2009). René Descartes pioneered the application of algebra to geometry by canonizing the following method: first express the problem by algebraic equations, then solve these equations by algebraic manipulations, and finish by translating these algebraic solutions back into geometrical terms. However, some mathematicians judged such use of algebra in geometry to be "rather far" from the problems at hand. A noteworthy example was Isaac Newton, despite his mastery of such application. As he wrote in his *Lucasian Lectures on Algebra*:

> Equations are expressions belonging to arithmetical computation and in geometry properly have no place except in so far as certain truly geometrical quantities (lines, surfaces and solids, that is, and their ratios) are stated to be equal to others. Multiplications, divisions and computations of that sort have recently been introduced into geometry, but the step is ill-considered and contrary to the original intentions of this science: for anyone who examines the constructions of problems by the straight line and circle devised by the first geometers will readily perceive that geometry was contrived as a means of escaping the tediousness of calculation by the ready drawing of lines. Consequently these two sciences [arithmetical computation and geometry] ought not to be confused. The Ancients so assiduously distinguished them one from the other that they never introduced arithmetical terms into geometry; while recent people, by confusing both, have lost the simplicity in which all elegance of geometry consists. (Newton 1972, p. 429)

While Newton thought algebra should not be part of geometrical proofs, he allowed a role for algebra in the *discovery* of new mathematical theorems. Here he drew on the classical distinction between the methods of synthesis and analysis (see Panza 1997). In an undated manuscript, Newton (2022) writes:

> The Ancients invented their Propositions by Analysis & Demonstrated them by synthesis, & admitted nothing into Geometry before it was demonstrated synthetically. I followed their example that the Propositions in that book might be admitted into Geometry. For the glory of Geometry is its certainty & nothing is to be admitted into Geometry before it be made as certain plane & evident as art can make it.

The importance of synthetic demonstrations in geometry, to be given in purely geometrical rather than algebraic terms, is for Newton also a matter of their *certainty*. He seems to have judged the deductive logical structure of Euclidean-style demonstrations from first principles to have the power to convince their readers with certainty of their conclusions, whereas analysis is only capable of showing how to discover a synthetic proof.

Descartes too saw a role for the methodological distinction between analysis and synthesis. His procedure for geometrical problem solving reflected this duality, requiring firstly the translation of the geometrical problem into algebraic language, then carrying out algebraic manipulations without regard for their geometrical content in order to find quantities that could be used to solve the original geometrical problem, and finally demanding the geometrical construction of these quantities in a way that could be expressed as a classical Euclidean-style synthetic proof. But Descartes and Newton differed about the epistemic significance of these two steps. While Newton insisted that only the synthetic, purely geometrical proof gave certainty of the theorem thereby proved, Descartes emphasized the knowledge given by the algebraic discovery. In his published work he gave almost no attention to synthesis.

However, this move away from purity came with a new understanding of the branches of mathematics whose boundaries purity was meant to respect. In *La géométrie*, Descartes (1902) characterized the ancients' support for purity as a result of their ignorance of deeper mathematical unities:

> Here I beg you to note in passing that the hesitation of the ancients to use arithmetic terms in geometry, which could only proceed from not seeing their relation clearly enough, caused a great deal of obscurity and difficulty in the way they explained themselves. (p. 378)

In a letter to Mersenne two years later, he explained that the link between algebra and geometry was even more profound: "Those who know the conjunction that is between geometry and arithmetic, cannot doubt that all one can do by arithmetic can also be done by geometry; but to want to make this understood to whose who conceive of them as completely distinct sciences, this would be a waste of time [*oleum et operam perdere*]" (February 9, 1639; see Descartes 1898, p. 504).

Descartes seems to have thought that he had uncovered the unity of algebra and geometry, but that this unity eluded explanation in any terms that could be understood by a doubter. If Descartes is right, the application of algebra to geometry is in fact pure, for algebra and geometry belong ultimately to one and the same branch of mathematics. This will be a recurring theme: pushes for impurity rest on cases for unification, and so, ironically, are pushes for purity within a mathematics sufficiently reconceptualized. We will return to this in Section 3.2.

The Cartesian application of algebra to geometry presaged a lively debate in the nineteenth century on purity in geometry to which we now turn. On one side of this debate were those who wanted to continue mixing algebra and geometry. For instance, Joseph-Louis Lagrange wrote that "as long as algebra and geometry have been separated, their progress has been slow and their usages limited; but when these two sciences are united, they have lent each other strength and have advanced together rapidly towards perfection" (see Lagrange 1876, p. 271). Lagrange's view was the by-now widespread view that impure methods in geometry afforded considerable gains in simplicity and efficiency, and were valuable for this reason. Joseph Gergonne and Julius Plücker were two other geometers advocating this side of the debate, as discussed by Jemma Lorenat in Lorenat (2015). We will return to this view in Section 4.5.

On the other side of this debate were those who took the point that pure methods in geometry have their particular advantages, as a reason to advocate for purity in geometry. Two representatives of this side are Michel Chasles and Jacob Steiner; Nicolas Michel discusses Chasles' stance in Michel (2020), and Lorenat discusses Steiner's in Lorenat (2016). Another was Sylvestre-François Lacroix, whose textbook on the differential and integral calculus was translated into English by Charles Babbage, John Herschel, and George Peacock, thereby playing an essential role in bringing British mathematics up to date with what had been happening abroad (see Fisch 1999). In this text Lacroix (1797) writes:

> Do not believe that by thus insisting on the advantages of algebraic analysis, I want to put synthesis and geometric analysis on trial. I think, on the contrary, that we neglect too much today the study of the ancients; but I would not want to mix, as one does in almost all works [today], geometrical considerations with algebraic calculations; it would be better, it seems to me, if each of these ways of doing things were carried out in separate treatises, as far as it can go; and if the results of both were to clarify each other, corresponding, so to speak, to the text of a book and its translation. (p. xxvi)

Lacroix maintains that algebra and geometry should be developed and used separately even if they can be translated between one another. Their mutual translatability was no longer contested, and as a consequence each could shed light on the other, but each domain should remain its own discipline with its own methods.

A pair of British geometers in the 1930s framed this debate in political terms:

> Those on the extreme right would not admit that any proof of a geometrical theorem by algebraic methods was a valid proof, though they admitted that these methods might be used to suggest problems for the pure geometer. Those on the extreme left did not indeed condemn the methods of Pure Geometry as invalid, but they certainly despised them as elephantine. (See O'Hara and Ward 1937, p. 3)

They continue by noting that this debate had practical consequences:

> An interesting example of the division of opinion is shown in the editorial policies of two of the leading mathematical journals of a century or more ago. *Crelle's Journal* would never admit to its pages any algebraic proof of a geometrical theorem; *Liouville's Journal*, on the other hand, refused to print anything but algebraic proofs of geometrical theorems. (*Ibid.*, p. 3.)

A recent monograph by Massimo Mazzotti has shown how a group of Neapolitan mathematicians in the early nineteenth century advocated for the separation of geometry from algebraic analysis, prioritizing the kind of knowledge engendered by the former, as part of a wider social, political and economic reaction against French revolutionary politics (see Mazzotti 2023).

Another political take on the geography of mathematics and purity as a preference for what is local emerges in the search for a pure proof of the fundamental theorem of algebra. John Dawson (2006) remarks that the search for proofs of this result about roots of polynomial equations "that aim to minimize the use of analytical or topological concepts" is an example of a purity project (p. 279). The mathematician Helmut Hasse (1930) discussed this case in an article on what he called "the new algebraic method." He described this method as "the striving *to reduce a given area of mathematics to its most general and therefore simplest conceptual foundation elements and to construct and extend it with their help alone*" (p. 20). He adds that "every mathematical discipline has *a certain fundamental attitude* of a philosophical nature that need not be spelled out but is nevertheless decisive for the character and development of the discipline." Each branch of mathematics has its own identity, and the algebraic method requires that we prove its truths from foundations of that branch alone. In this way, Hasse's algebraic method seems to encapsulate the search for purity.

To illustrate his algebraic method, Hasse turns to the solution of rational algebraic equations. The "natural means" for solving such equations, he says, are the usual algebraic operations, but the classical theory "goes outside the realm of these natural means...it enters the realm of complex numbers and uses aids from analysis to prove the so-called fundamental theorem of algebra...[drawing on] the essentially new concept of limit" (p. 19). The modern algebraic method critiques and seeks to remedy this, by removing the reliance on analysis. He lauds the work of Emil Artin and Otto Schreier on real-closed fields as having accomplished this:

> Now if there exists a development [*Aufbau*] of the theory of algebraic equations that eschews the limit concept and relies solely on the elementary arithmetic operations, then such a development must, of course, be preferred to others. Such a development, with the additional qualities of clarity and simplicity, relies on abstract field theory...[and] has actually been done by Artin and Schreier. [By their work] real algebra and the fundamental theorem of algebra regain their citizenship rights [*Bürgerrecht*] in algebra. (Hasse 1930, p. 20)

This last phrase, "citizenship rights," resonated in 1930s Germany. Hasse himself was a conservative who would become a Nazi sympathizer (and perhaps party member) in Göttingen and Berlin.

In the Nazi era in Germany there was a movement of "Deutsche Mathematik," led by world-class mathematicians like Ludwig Bieberbach and Oswald Teichmüller, identifying talents for particular branches of mathematics with racial archetypes and "denigrat[ing] nongeometric mathematics, especially algebra, as insufficiently *völkisch*" (see Segal 2003, p. 489). As Sanford Segel documents, Bieberbach's Nazi-era journal *Deutsche Mathematik* would publish about three times as many pure geometry articles as related journals like *Mathematische Annalen* (29 percent versus 10.8 percent of the articles published and 31.3 percent versus 10.1 percent of the pages of these journals) while only a third as many articles in impure geometry, mixed with analysis, topology or algebra (2.4 percent versus 6.4 percent of the articles and 2.9 percent versus 6.0 percent of the pages). "It seems fair to say," writes Segal, "that the density of geometry articles in *Deutsche Mathematik* is roughly twice that of the other journals, and the geometry is far more 'pure'."

Each issue of the first volume of *Deutsche Mathematik*, in 1936, started with a page containing only a quotation. As Segal notes (p. 394), two issues started with the same quote from Kant: "Foreign words betray either poverty, which must be concealed, or negligence" (*AA* XV, p. 369). One of these two issues, number 4, included a laudatory note for the avowed Nazi Theodor Vahlen written by Friedrich Engel, whose interest in purity we discussed in Section 1 (see Segal 2003, p. 396). The historian of ideas John Theodore Merz (1903), in his essay on the development of mathematics in the nineteenth century, remarked on the connection between German preferences for linguistic purity and mathematical purity:

> In this way the great geometrician, Jacob Steiner, *e.g.*, refused the assistance of analysis in the solution of geometrical problems, conceiving geometry as a complete organism which should solve its problems by its own means....Mathematical rigorists in this sense would look upon the use of mixed methods or operations not belonging to the same group with that kind of disfavor with which we should regard an essayist who could not express his ideas in pure English, but was obliged to import foreign words and expressions. It is interesting to see that the country which has offended most by the importation of foreign words—namely, Germany—is that in which this purism in mathematical taste has found the most definite expression. (p. 632)

The linguist Deborah Cameron (1995) has given the name "verbal hygiene" to the desire to police language use for failure to adhere to norms such as avoiding foreign terms inasmuch as is possible. In Arana and Burnett (2023) we have begun to investigate the parallel highlighted by Merz between verbal hygiene and what we call "mathematical hygiene," the desire to police mathematical practices for failure to adhere to norms such as purity and explanatoriness. In both cases we can look at the reasons offered for such policing and observe the role of ideologies in their justification.

Anand Pillay (2021) has noted the ideological associations with purity:

> In the background, and related to purity of methods, is the notion of "authenticity" (of a topic, subject, method, in mathematics). "Authenticity" has an identity politics connotation, where it is about using the right words, or slogans, by which the faithful can recognize one another and exclude those who do not belong. (p. 194)

Pillay says he prefers the term "integrity" for this pursuit, "where one seeks the essential mathematical content and ideas and tries to avoid too much mixing up of notions which are only superficially connected." Pillay's word choices remind us that the language we use for our reasons for norms such as purity matter: that the associations these norms have with wider ideologies may give us additional reasons to pursue these norms, or to eschew them.

Continuing on from this sociopolitical interlude, we return to purity in geometry in the nineteenth century. There is a third side of this debate that was not then widely taken, but finds amongst its adherents L. E. J. Brouwer a little later: the view that Descartes seemed to come to, that geometry had been arithmetized and thus that no principled line can be drawn between pure geometry and algebraic geometry. As Brouwer (1913) put it, "since Descartes we have learned to reduce all these geometries to arithmetic by means of the calculus of coordinates" (p. 86). On this view, the coordinate methods characteristic of applications of algebra to geometry are, against appearances, pure, because geometry is *reducible* to the arithmetic of coordinates. How this reduction should be understood will concern us again later as we reflect on the significance of set-theoretic reductions for purity.

The debate on purity in the nineteenth century thus raised a rich variety of philosophical problems, involving epistemology, semantics, ontology, and methodology, among others. It is no wonder, then, that it played a role in the turn to foundations during the nineteenth and twentieth centuries, to which we now turn.

Bernard Bolzano's work on the foundations of analysis involved purity, notably in his search for a nongeometric proof of the intermediate value theorem of real analysis. This theorem says that for a real function $f$ continuous on a closed bounded interval $[a, b]$, for every $\mu$ such that $f(a) < \mu < f(b)$, there is a $v$ such that $a < v < b$, with $f(v) = \mu$. Bolzano objected, in particular, to the use of the following proposition to prove this theorem: every continuous line of simple curvature of which some ordinate values are positive and some negative must intersect the $x$-axis at a point between the positive and negative ordinate values. He described this as a "truth borrowed from geometry," and he regarded the borrowing as illicit. He explained himself as follows:

> It is ... an intolerable offense against *correct method* to derive truths of *pure* (or general) mathematics (i.e. arithmetic, algebra, analysis) from considerations which belong to a merely *applied* (or special) part, namely, *geometry.* Indeed, have we not felt and recognized for a long time the incongruity of such *metabasis eis allo genos*? Have we not already avoided this whenever possible in hundreds of other cases, and regarded this avoidance as a merit? ... [I]f one considers that the proofs of the science should not merely be *certainty-makers* [Gewissmachungen], but rather *groundings* [Begründungen], i.e. presentations of the objective reason for the truth concerned, then it is self-evident that the strictly scientific proof, or the objective reason, of a truth which holds equally for *all* quantities, whether in space or not, cannot possibly lie in a truth which holds merely for quantities which are in *space*. (See Bolzano 1999, p. 228, with slightly modified translation from Detlefsen and Arana 2011, pp. 4–5)

Bolzano's epistemology of mathematics was thus Aristotelian in character, identifying the best, "scientific" proofs in mathematics as those proceeding from objective grounds, and preserving the Aristotelian injunction against impurity (see Detlefsen 2008 and Detlefsen 2010 for more detailed treatments of Bolzano on purity). Bolzano's quest for purity was thus part of his foundational project, concerning not only the proper organizational of mathematical domains, but also the quality of knowledge resulting from proofs in systems so organized.

Among Bolzano's readers was the mathematician Richard Dedekind, who followed Bolzano in seeking purity in his pursuit of the foundations of mathematics. In his work on the foundations of real analysis, Dedekind stressed that "I demand that arithmetic shall develop out of itself," noting that "comparisons with non-arithmetical notions have furnished the immediate occasion for the extension of the number-concept...but this is certainly no reason for introducing these foreign notions [*fremden*] into arithmetic itself, the science of numbers" (see Dedekind 1872, p. 771). In a letter to Rudolf Lipschitz dated October 6, 1876, he insists that he can develop the arithmetic of the real numbers "without any interference of foreign things [*fremdartiger Dinge*]" (see Dedekind 1932, p. 470). Here Dedekind echoed Bolzano, in looking to extrude foreign notions, especially geometrical notions, from the foundations of analysis. Instead, he sought a purely arithmetical theory of real number, noting that "every theorem of algebra and higher analysis, no matter how remote, can be expressed as a theorem about natural numbers – a declaration I have heard repeatedly from the lips of Dirichlet" (see Dedekind 1888, translation from Ewald 1999, p. 792).

Dedekind's reference to Dirichlet is consistent with Dirichlet's pursuit of an arithmetic proof of Jacobi's four squares theorem that we saw in Section 1. But Dirichlet was not interested in purity in the way Dedekind was. We remarked in Section 1 that Dirichlet wanted to make Jacobi's purely arithmetic proof simpler. He did not indicate that he saw particular value in the pursuit of purity otherwise. Indeed, Wilfried Sieg has problematized Dirichlet's interest in purity, noting that he lauded the merit of impurity in number theory (see Ferreirós and Gray 2006, p. 342). This illustrates that one can value both purity and impurity, for different reasons. As we will discuss later, the fact that theorems admit multiple proofs mean that we can hold opposing values in our proving practices, sometimes favoring one value, sometimes another.

Dedekind also worked to find a pure proof of the Riemann–Roch theorem, which his friend Riemann had proved using the topological concept of continuity in the form of the Dirichlet principle (see Arana 2007). With Heinrich Weber, Dedekind showed in 1882 how to express the Riemann–Roch theorem in algebraic terms, involving fields of algebraic functions defined on a Riemann surface, itself thought of algebraically. Applying Dedekind's ideal-theoretic approach to algebraic number theory, Dedekind and Weber were able to give a purely algebraic proof of the Riemann–Roch theorem. Dedekind and Weber thus achieved an algebraic proof of an algebraic theorem, but doing so required a reconceptualization of the Riemann–Roch theorem as an algebraic theorem. We will see further examples of such conceptual transformations of theorems in the pursuit of purity.

Gottlob Frege's understanding of purity echoed Bolzano's, even if his application of it was quite different. In the *Grundlagen*, Frege (1980) identified some proofs of theorems as "the ultimate ground upon which rests the justification for holding it to be true" (§3). He believed that these "canonical" proofs of arithmetic truths would show the intimate connection of arithmetic and logic. If we can show that arithmetic is logic, he says, we will have identified "the kind of ground on which their proof rests" (§17). On this, he quotes Leibniz's (1996) *Nouveaux Essais*: such proofs show "the connexion and natural order of truths, which is always the same" (IV.7). In order to reveal such an objective order of truths, proofs of arithmetic theorems must be purified of geometrical content. Frege (1984) explained that the "reluctance" of mathematicians to accept complex numbers was

> facilitated by geometrical interpretations; but with these, something foreign was introduced into arithmetic. Inevitably there arose the desire of once again extruding these geometrical aspects. It appeared contrary to all reason that purely arithmetical theorems should rest on geometrical axioms; and it was inevitable that proofs which apparently established such a dependence should seem to obscure the true state of affairs. The task of deriving what was arithmetical by purely arithmetical means, i.e. purely logically, could not be put off. (pp. 116–117)

Frege's logicist program was thus also a programmatic call for purity.

Purity remains a concern to contemporary mathematicians. During the nineteenth century, algebraic geometers became interested in the following question: given an algebraic surface, characterize the families of surfaces that intersect the given surface in curves of particular kinds. Geometers made progress on the case when these families of surfaces formed a kind of linearly dependent system. As Babbitt and Goodstein (2011) explains, in 1905 Federigo Enriques, a member of the celebrated school of Italian algebraic geometry, gave a complete characterization of such families of surfaces intersecting a given smooth algebraic surface in an irreducible and continuous system of curves. He did not find his proof satisfying, however, because it was not purely geometric. As he put it in a piece written with Enrico Castelnuovo, another member of this school:

> We have not succeeded in demonstrating this theorem using geometric methods…This result is therefore the fruit of a long series of researches, to which the transcendental methods of M. Picard and the geometrical methods used in Italy contributed equally. (See Picard and Simart 1906, pp. 489, 495; Gray 2012, p. 503)

In fact, Enriques had not succeeded even in that; his proof was wrong, as discovered by Severi in 1921, who then gave a new proof that was quickly seen to be incorrect. A correct proof, entirely transcendental, had in the meantime been given by Poincaré.

In a 1945 letter to Corrado Segre, looking back on these developments, Castelnuovo lamented, "we would need to have a fully satisfying geometrical demonstration" (see Babbitt and Goodstein 2011, p. 246). The historians Aldo Brigaglia and Ciro Cilberto (1995) have stressed that Castelnuovo and Enriques' dissatisfaction with Enriques' transcendental proof was for "philosophical reasons":

> In fact, for Enriques and Severi, who were postulating a central role for the projective algebro-geometric methods in mathematics, the missing resolution of such an essential problem in the theory of surfaces – which they considered as their creation – was always an unacceptable humiliation. Thus they repeatedly returned to the consideration of this problem, even if they never were definitively successful in resolving it. (p. 47)

In 1966 David Mumford gave a purely algebraic-geometric proof of the result, using methods developed by Jean-Pierre Serre, Alexandre Grothendieck, and Kunihiko Kodaira, thus finally meeting the purity challenge (see Toffoli and Fontanari (2023) for another angle on this episode).

Purity concerns have also abounded in contemporary number theory. In the next section we will discuss the use of complex analysis in proving the prime number theorem. Here we discuss another celebrated example of impurity. Andrew Wiles' proof of Fermat's Last Theorem has attracted considerable attention for the distance between its simple arithmetic statement and its difficult, varied proof. Like Jacobi's work a century earlier, Wiles' proof is in part an application of elliptic functions (more precisely, elliptic curves), with additional methods from algebraic geometry. Israel Kleiner (2012) underlines the distance between its conclusion and its methods, noting that "the problem belongs to number theory – a question about positive integers. But what area does the proof come from? It is unlikely one could give a satisfactory answer, for the proof brings together many important areas – a characteristic of recent mathematics" (p. 60).

Wiles' proof electrified the world, both for the historical significance of the theorem, but also for the spectacle of the distance between its conclusion and its methods. A notorious example of its reception in the media concerned columnist Marilyn vos Savant in *Parade* magazine, distributed freely with millions of Sunday newspapers each week in the USA until 2022. In her column of November 21, 1993, vos Savant wrote that Wiles hadn't succeeded, because it relied (in its work on modularity) on non-Euclidean methods that could be used to square the circle, a known impossibility. She elaborated in her book published that same year that Wiles' proof "isn't as satisfying as it could be" (vos Savant 1993, p. 60) because it "inhabits a very different world from the world inhabited by Fermat" (p. 16). Quoting a newspaper article featuring Simon Kochen, Wiles's department chair at Princeton at the time, she noted that Wiles "was throwing the kitchen sink at it, using all kinds of techniques that had been developed in recent years" (p. 17). Her book and her *Parade* column caused an outcry by mathematicians, and in response in an amended edition of her book in 1995 she stressed her view that we should try to "find a proof with Fermat's tools" (see Farrell, Farrell, and Rodgers 2016). Since Wiles's "kitchen sink" proof drew on so many elements alien to Fermat's world, it would be better, she maintained, to a find a proof closer to the theorem as understood by Fermat.

Stripping away the misunderstandings and confusions, vos Savant's view is purist. Her view was put more succinctly by Colin McLarty, remarking that "Fermat's Last Theorem is just about numbers, so it seems like we ought to be able to prove it by just talking about numbers" (cf. University 2013). The quest for a pure proof of Fermat's Last Theorem resonates with the impression that number theory to date has no statements that cannot be proved purely, an impression that has been studied by mathematical logicians. Jeremy Avigad states Harvey Friedman's "grand conjecture," that "every theorem published in the *Annals of Mathematics* whose statement involves only finitary mathematical objects (i.e. what logicians call an arithmetical statement) can be proved in elementary arithmetic" (see Avigad 2003), of which Fermat's Last Theorem is a special case. "Elementary arithmetic" here means a particular formal theory, in short, first-order Peano Arithmetic with induction limited to bounded formulas but with axioms asserting the totality of the exponentiation function. As Avigad discussed, considerable evidence for this conjecture exists in proof theory (see Arana 2014), but so far Fermat's Last Theorem has eluded it. Recently McLarty (2020) has made important progress toward this contemporary project in purity, showing that the Grothendieck universes deployed in Wiles' framework can be replaced with methods of the same logical strength as finite-order arithmetic.

For a final contemporary example, consider the Briançon–Skoda Theorem, an important result in algebraic geometry (see Briançon and Skoda 1974). Let $R$ be either the formal or convergent power series ring in $d$ variables and let $I$ be an ideal of $R$. Then $\overline{I^d} \subseteq I$, where $\overline{I}$ is the *integral closure* of an ideal $I$. Of this result, Joseph Lipman and Bernard Teissier (1981) remark: "The proof given by Briançon and Skoda of this completely algebraic statement is based on a quite transcendental deep result of Skoda. . . . The absence of an algebraic proof has been for algebraists something of a scandal – perhaps even an insult – and certainly a challenge" (p. 97).

Lipman and Teissier then give an algebraic proof satisfying the challenge. The "scandal ... insult ... challenge" here is, in our terms, an impure proof of a theorem for which, until then, no pure proof was known. Re-proving the theorem in a purely algebraic way merited publication in the excellent and mainstream *Michigan Mathematical Journal*.

In this section, then, we saw purity develop and transmute, in response to mathematical and philosophical developments. With Aristotle, we saw how an awareness of the geographicity of mathematics, in its division into branches, was reflected in his injunction against kind-crossing. Proclus' attention to the organization of Euclid's *Elements* highlighted a contrasting constraint, favoring proofs employing what is no less elementary than what is being proved. In what follows we will clarify these two conceptions of purity, on the one hand concerned with the identity of the topics being studied, on the other hand with the way statements are organized within a subject matter. In doing so, we will distinguish several different varieties of these broad types of purity that have occurred in practice.

## 3  Types of Purity

In the introduction to his textbook *Algèbre linéaire et géométrie élémentaire*, the Bourbakiste Jean Dieudonné (1969) advocated for purity in geometry in the following way.

> My last general remark concerns an aspect of modern Mathematics which is in a way complementary to its unifying tendencies; it concerns its capacity for sorting out features which have become unduly entangled. I am thinking above all of the distinction (which has been felt quite sharply since Poncelet) between the "affine" type of geometric properties and "metric" type of properties. From the logical standpoint, it is quite shocking to see these two types of properties mixed up in a proper hotch-potch since the days when traditional Euclidean geometry began. It is incredible that two such disparate concepts as that of parallelism and perpendicularity, to name but one example, should have been placed on the same plane. In linear algebra, this distinction emerges quite simply and naturally, the two types of property depending respectively on two groups of axioms which are quite separate from the very beginning. The results can then quite easily be developed, one apart from the other. It may well be that some will find this insistence on "purity" of the various lines of reasoning rather superfluous and pedantic; for my part, I feel that one must always try to *understand* what one is doing as well as one can and that it is good discipline for the mind to seek not only economy of means in working procedures but also to adapt hypotheses as closely to conclusions as is possible. (pp. 11–12)

Here Dieudonné is occupied with the distinction between affine geometry and metric geometry, wherein the former gives a central place to parallelism, and the latter, to distance. Geometers in the nineteenth century came to distinguish these two approaches and to see how much could be developed in each without the other. Dieudonné calls the mixing of these approaches "shocking," and promotes detangling them for reasons of understanding and mental discipline. We will discuss and evaluate reasons to value purity (and impurity) in Section 4. In this section, we want to make better sense of what purity is. In this passage Dieudonné says that it is a search for economy of means, means that are maximally "close" to what is being proved.

In suggesting that purity is a matter of distance between theorem and the means of proof, Dieudonné echoes the kinds of descriptions of it that we have seen so far: that a proof of a theorem is pure if it draws only on what is "close" or "intrinsic" to that theorem, or avoids what is "extrinsic," "extraneous," "distant," "remote," "alien," or "foreign" to what is being proved. But his description evokes different senses of purity that we should untangle. In one sense, the means of proof of a theorem are close to that theorem if they are contained in the theorem or belong to the branch of mathematics to which it belongs. In another sense, they are close if they are no stronger than what is being proved. This rough division of how purity can be understood will guide our work in this section.

## 3.1 Geographical Purity

In Section 2, we saw how purity can be formulated in terms of branches of mathematics. The classic formation of this kind is Aristotle's, writing that "we cannot, in demonstrating, pass from one genus to another. We cannot, for instance, prove geometrical truths by arithmetic." Accordingly, we can define a proof of a statement to be *geographically pure* if it draws only on what belongs to the branch of mathematics to which the statement belongs.

Several of the examples of purity we have already surveyed are of this type, like Jacobi's and Bolzano's. Ferraro and Panza (2012) have studied a case of what we call geographic purity in Lagrange's theory of analytic functions. Lagrange sought to prove theorems of the infinitesimal calculus using only "an algebraic, purely formal theory centered on the manipulation of (finite or infinite) polynomials through the method of indeterminate coefficients" (p. 96). He sought algebraic solutions for what he understood to be algebraic problems, rather than those using principles of infinitesimals "foreign to the spirit of analysis, which should have no metaphysics but that which consists in the first principles and in the fundamental operations of calculation" (see Lagrange 1799, p. 233, translation from Ferraro and Panza 2012, p. 97).

Talk of purity in number theory is often geographical. We can illustrate this with an example that we will have reason to revisit. Legendre and Gauss hypothesized that the number of primes up to an integer $n$, $\pi(n)$, is approximately $\frac{n}{\log n}$, but they did not prove it. The path to a proof opened with Euler's clever proof of the infinitude of primes, observing that when $s = 1$, $\sum_{n \geq 1} \frac{1}{n^s} = \prod_p \frac{1}{1 - p^{-s}}$. Suppose there are finitely many primes; then the product is finite but the sum, the harmonic series, diverges. The infinitude of primes follows by contradiction. Riemann built on Euler's work, using the identity just described to define his "zeta" function, $\zeta(s) := \sum_{n \geq 1} \frac{1}{n^s}$. This sum converges absolutely for real-valued $s > 1$, and Riemann showed, by powerful new methods, how to extend it to complex-valued $s \neq 1$ (that is, to numbers $s = a + bi$, where $i = \sqrt{-1}$, and $a$ and $b$ are real numbers). Riemann's work entailed, again by complex analysis, that Legendre and Gauss' hypothesis regarding the number of primes less than an integer $n$ is equivalent to the nonexistence of zeros of $\zeta(s)$ on the line $\mathrm{Re}(s) = 1$. Hadamard and de la Vallée Poussin proved the latter, independently, in 1896, using Riemann's powerful complex-analytic methods. Thus Legendre and Gauss' hypothesis is now called the *prime number theorem*.

These complex-analytic proofs irked some number theorists. For instance, A. E. Ingham (1932) remarked that "the solution just outlined may be held to be unsatisfactory in that it introduces ideas very remote from the original problem, and it is natural to ask for a proof of the prime number theorem not depending on the theory of a complex variable" (pp. 5–6). Bram Pel (2023) has shown how concern about the use of imaginary numbers in solving real-valued integrals marked a dispute between Pierre-Simon Laplace and Siméon-Denis Poisson in the early nineteenth century. We will comment a little later on the "elementary" proofs of the prime number theorem found by Atle Selberg and Paul Erdős, independently in 1949 – a discovery deemed important enough that it contributed to Selberg's winning a Fields Medal in 1950. For now, we remark that the search for a pure proof of the prime number theorem is sometimes expressed geographically. For instance, Harold Davenport (2008) writes:

> We have already said that the proof of Dirichlet's Theorem on primes in arithmetical progressions and the proof of the prime number theorem were analytical, and made use of methods which cannot be said to belong properly to the theory of numbers. The propositions themselves relate entirely to the natural numbers, and it seems reasonable that they should be provable without the intervention of such foreign ideas. (p. 27)

Geographicity emerges in the talk of what "belongs properly to" and what is "foreign to" the discipline of number theory.

We have adapted the term "geographical" from Jean-Michel Salanskis' work on the "geographicity of mathematics," already introduced in the previous section. Salanskis (2008) observes that mathematics has always been and continues to be divided into branches, but also that this division is "as shifting and relative as the map of Europe or of the world" (p. 175). Even as the ancient division of mathematics into arithmetic and geometry is reflected today in the distinction between discrete and continuous mathematics, mathematics today admits more fine-grained divisions. According to the Mathematics Subject Classification 2020, designed by the American Mathematical Society and zbMATH Open (formerly Zentralblatt MATH), mathematics has more than sixty branches, including number theory, algebra, analysis, and geometry, but also branches that mix other branches, for example algebraic geometry and analytic number theory.

The landscape of branches of contemporary mathematics sets limits on the usefulness of geographical purity. Firstly, results belonging to several branches that mark movement toward new fused branches do not by themselves pose obstacles to the search for purity. As we saw in the previous section, algebraic geometers can seek purity, avoiding analytic or topological means, for example. Poincaré's uniformization theorem – that every simply connected Riemann surface is conformally equivalent to one of three Riemann surfaces: the open unit disk, the complex plane, or the Riemann sphere – belongs at once to algebraic topology, differential geometry, and complex analysis. A geographically pure proof of uniformization would draw on these branches but not others. But these branches comprise a great deal of mathematics, and one might wonder about the use of such a broad and tolerant notion of purity. An advocate for the unity of mathematics in which the boundaries between branches have been forgotten might say that they too advocate purity: mathematical proofs for mathematical theorems, nothing more. This wide conception of purity is far from the fine-grained distinctions characteristic of historical purity discriminations. Yet, as we have seen, mathematicians continue to make those fine-grained distinctions.

Another concern for the local shows further limits of geographical purity. A researcher might want to use only part of a particular discipline to prove a result. For example, consider the infinitude of primes theorem: that for all natural numbers, there exists a greater prime number. The classical Euclidean proof from *Elements* IX.20 is purely arithmetic and is thus geographically pure. Let us consider, though, an investigator who wants to prove the theorem without addition, seeing it as extraneous. Neither primality nor the infinitude of natural numbers seems to make use of addition. A prime number is a number divisible only by 1 and itself, and divisibility is not an additive notion. As for infinitude, this rests on an ordering, which is also not an additive notion; simply thinking of the numbers as following in discrete succession from 1 generates the ordering, but the unary successor operation is not the full binary operation of addition. This is a purity project, but not a geographical one, because the geographic conception does not allow for such fine-grained distinctions within mathematical branches. The infinitude of primes is an arithmetic theorem, and arithmetic includes addition as a basic operation. To make sense of this purity project, we will need another conception of purity.

One might riposte that the multiplicative fragment of arithmetic is its own discipline, studied by logicians as Skolem arithmetic. This purity project could thus be framed geographically as the search for a proof of the infinitude of primes in Skolem arithmetic. But one would be hard-pressed to find the study of this fragment of arithmetic outside of mathematical logic. From the point of view of school children and number theorists alike, Skolem arithmetic is a curio rather than a branch of mathematics. Framing this purity project in terms of geometrical purity seems to require taking a stance on the question of what it takes to count as a branch of mathematics, a question that may strike us as merely terminological.

## 3.2 Topical Purity

An example from geometry will point the way toward another conception of purity better suited to these cases that geographical purity does not handle well. The Sylvester–Gallai theorem says "that in any configuration of $n$ points in the plane, not all on a line, there is a line which contains exactly two of the points" (Aigner and Ziegler 2010, p. 63). H. S. M. Coxeter (1948) sought a proof of this result that avoided metric notions, remarking that "it seems to me that parallelism and distance are essentially foreign to this problem, which is concerned only with incidence and order" (p. 27). Coxeter (1989) acknowledged that metric notions belong to geometry, observing that "etymologically, 'geometry without measurement' looks like a contradiction in terms" (p. 176). On a geographic conception of purity, Coxeter's purity project looks badly framed, like our arithmetician looking for a nonadditive proof of the infinitude of primes. But Coxeter (1989) insisted that the concept of straight line is not a metrical notion as some would understand it, as the shortest distance between two points, but rather as an *ordinal* notion. He notes that what he calls Euclid's "famous definition," that "a line (segment) is that which lies evenly between its ends ... suggests the possibility of regarding intermediacy as a primitive concept and using it to define a line segment as the set of all points between two given points" (p. 176). Thus did Coxeter justify his view that the

Sylvester–Gallai theorem "is concerned only with incidence and order," and his concomitant successful search for a purely incidence and order-theoretic proof of it (see Arana 2008, p. 39, and Arana 2009, pp. 4–5).

As with the previous case, we can try to frame Coxeter's quest geographically. Indeed, Coxeter called his fragment of geometry "ordered geometry," following earlier work of Pasch, Veblen, and Hilbert; in the latter's *Grundlagen der Geometrie*, ordered geometry corresponds to the first two groups of axioms taken together. As with Skolem arithmetic, though, ordered geometry does not attract much interest besides that of logically-inclined geometers (see Pambuccian 2009 and Pambuccian 2011).

We can avoid a decision on whether ordered geometry is genuinely a branch of mathematics by following a methodological suggestion of Hilbert and adopting another conception of purity. In his 1900 address in Paris to the International Congress of Mathematicians, Hilbert (1901) claimed that in solving a mathematical problem we ought to use only the conceptual resources used in stating that problem:

> It remains to discuss briefly what general requirements may be justly laid down for the solution of a mathematical problem. I should say first of all, this: that it shall be possible to establish the correctness of the solution by means of a finite number of steps based upon a finite number of hypotheses which lie in the presentation of the problem and which must always be exactly formulated. (p. 257)

In lectures given shortly before the Paris address, Hilbert (2004) emphasized his view of purity in explaining his search for a purely planar projective proof of the planar Desargues theorem (compare Arana and Mancosu 2012):

> This theorem gives us an opportunity now to discuss an important issue. *The content [Inhalt] of Desargues' theorem belongs completely to planar geometry; for its proof we needed to use space.* Therefore we are for the first time in a position to put into practice *a critique of means of proof.* In modern mathematics such criticism is raised very often, where the aim is to preserve *the purity of method [die Reinheit der Methode]*, i.e. to prove theorems if possible using means that are suggested by the content of the theorem. (pp. 315–316)

Thus Hilbert judged a proof to be pure just in case it draws only upon what is "suggested by the content of the theorem" being proved, or on what "lies in" the presentation of the problem being solved; or, perhaps better, inasmuch as it stays as close as possible to the conceptual resources used in *understanding* that theorem or problem. Since he judged that the "content of Desargues' theorem belongs completely to planar geometry," he maintained that a three-dimensional proof of it is impure in his sense. (See also Hilbert 1971, pp. 106–107, where Hilbert calls purity a form of the "ground rule" of his method in this work.)

From Hilbert's views we may extract the conception of purity we may call "topical." Following Hilbert's *fin de siècle* stress on problems, we focus on topically pure solutions to problems rather than solely on proofs of theorems. We reprise here from Detlefsen and Arana (2011) the representation of problems by ordered triples $\mathcal{P} = (?_{y/n}, P, \phi)$, where '$?_{y/n}$' stands for a "yes-no" *interrogative attitude*; '$P$' stands for a propositional content; and '$\phi$' stands for a *formulation* of $P$. A problem is the subject of an investigation by what we will refer to as an *investigator*, though an investigator need not be an individual human person, but could be a community of some sort. A formulation is the means by which an investigator represents a content to herself. For example, a community of English-speaking number theorists may ask whether every even number greater than 3 is equal to the sum of two prime numbers – that is, they may seek a resolution to the Goldbach Conjecture. In so doing, they take a yes-no interrogative attitude to the content of this problem, formulated in mathematical English.

We call the *topic* of a problem the family of commitments that together determine what its content is for a given investigator. These are the definitions, axioms, and inferences such that if the investigator were to stop accepting any one of them, then the content of the problem would not be what it is for her. That is to say, the problem whose solution she had been seeking would no longer be the object of her investigation. To put the point epistemically, their understanding of the problem would be thereby changed. For example, if the aforementioned number theory community were to rescind their commitment that every natural number has a successor, then they would no longer understand the natural numbers as an indefinitely extended sequence. Were this the case, the Goldbach Conjecture would no longer have the same content as it did for this community, since it would concern instead a finite sequence. By contrast, if this community stopped accepting that every rectangle has four right angles, the content of the Goldbach Conjecture would remain unchanged for them. Thus the axiom that every natural number has a successor belongs to the topic of the Goldbach Conjecture for this investigator, but the definition of a rectangle as a four-sided polygon with four right angles does not.

Our talk of rescinding commitments in mathematics may strike some as odd. After all, we are talking about commitments to axioms, definitions, and rules of inference, matters which seem to be "foundational." Yet such rescinding is a feature of mathematical life, even if in times of stability it is infrequent. Minor changes in definitions are common, particularly as a concept is being isolated; think of the changes in the definition of group surveyed in Wussing (2007).

With the rise of non-Euclidean geometry, the geometry community rescinded their uniform commitment to the parallel postulate, admitting it thereafter as marking a special domain of geometry, that of Euclidean geometry. Rules of inference too can be rescinded, as the case of Hermann Weyl's time as an intuitionist shows (compare van Dalen 1995). Indeed, for a commitment to earn its name, it must be something that is held but whose holding, at least implicitly, requires agency; and such agency can be employed in differing ways.

The upshot of this analytic work is that we can now introduce another conception of purity. A solution of a problem is *topically pure* if it draws only on what belongs to the topic of the problem. This makes sharper Hilbert's view that purity concerns solutions that use only "means that are suggested by the content of the theorem," the theorem whose proof constitutes a solution to a problem under investigation.

Topical purity differs from geographical purity in that it limits what is pure to what is contained within the problem's topic, rather than to the entire branch to which the problem (or theorem) belongs. In that way, topical purity is a "local" purity constraint. We can then make sense of purity attributions where the object of the investigation seems itself mixed. For instance, Poincaré's uniformization theorem says that every simply connected Riemann surface is conformally equivalent to one of three Riemann surfaces: the open unit disk, the complex plane, or the Riemann sphere. Uniformization belongs to each of algebraic topology, differential geometry, and complex analysis, at minimum, because Riemann surfaces are at once topological, geometrical, analytic, and algebraic. No sense can be made of a geographical purity attribution for uniformization, since it would require some single branch of mathematics containing all these subjects that does not simply flatten their differences into some indistinct unity. But the topic of uniformization entails no such difficulty, since a topic need not be identified with any existing branch. On the topical conception, then, it becomes intelligible to talk of a pure proof of uniformization – the search for which, we would claim, helps makes sense of Poincaré's work on the problem during the almost thirty-year period that the problem occupied him (see Saint-Gervais (2010) for a detailed telling of this result's story).

Instances of topical purity abound. We saw it in Section 1 in Einstein's example from elementary geometry, where he remarked that "we are completely satisfied only if we feel of each intermediate concept that it has to do with the proposition to be proved." Here Einstein localized his search for purity to the proposition being proved, adding that impurity arises in his first proof when it "uses an auxiliary line which has nothing to do with the content of the proposition to be proved."

We can also look to number theory for examples of topical purity. Let's look again at the infinitude of primes, or for short, IP (recapitulating a longer discussion in Arana 2014). Its topic includes definitions and axioms for the natural numbers with an ordering, and primality. The wider public, as well as number theorists, understands the natural numbers to begin with a first number 1, followed by other numbers that are understood to be the successors of the numbers that came before. These suppositions can be codified by axioms for successor and an induction axiom, following Poincaré's argument that induction is essential to understanding the natural numbers (see Poincaré 1902). The ordering induced by successor is normally understood as linear and discrete, and axioms specifying these too can be added. Finally, a natural number is normally understood as prime if it is greater than 1 and only divisible by 1 and itself, so in addition to adding this definition to the topic of IP, we must add axioms defining divisibility.

At this point we could stop, taking the topic as determined for an investigator for whom divisibility is basic. We can understand such an investigator as capable of assessing whether one natural number is divisible by another, for instance by a combinatorial understanding of whether particular finite collections can be partitioned into a certain number of partitions. Or we could continue, from the perspective of an investigator who understands divisibility in terms of multiplication: A number $a$ is divisible by another $b$ if there is a number $c$ such that $c$ multiplied by $b$ is $a$. In the latter case, the topic of IP would also include axioms for multiplication. These are two different topics and we need not choose between them, because each corresponds to a different investigator. There is no single answer to the question of what a problem's or theorem's topic is.

A first candidate for a topically pure proof of IP is the classical Euclidean proof. If $a = 1$, then since $2 = S(1)$ is prime, where $S$ is the successor function, we know that there is a prime greater than $a = 1$. So, suppose that $a > 1$. Let $p_1, p_2, \ldots, p_n$ be all the primes less than or equal to $a$, and let $Q = S(p_1 \cdot p_2 \cdots p_n)$. Then $Q$ has a prime divisor $b$ that is not equal to any of the $p_i$, and so $b > a$. For our investigator who takes multiplication to be part of IP's topic, this proof is, at first glance, topically pure. It makes no use of addition and so makes sense of the purity project we discussed in the last section as falling outside the scope of geographical purity.

For our investigator who does not include multiplication, however, the matter is more complex. The classical proof uses multiplication to compute $Q$, so this proof is not topically pure for our nonmultiplicative investigator. We are aware of no simple purely divisibility-theoretic proof of IP. Cegielski has worked on axiomatic theories of the arithmetic of divisibility (see Cegielski 1984, Cegielski, Matijasevich, and Richard 1996), but these theories include IP as an axiom. A more promising approach was developed by Julia Robinson in Robinson (1949). She defines multiplication in terms of just successor and divisibility; using this definition, we can translate the classical proof of IP into a topically pure proof (according to our multiplico-centric investigator). Robinson noted that this "mechanical" translation will yield a proof from arithmetic axioms that are "complicated and artificial" (pp. 102–103), notably longer than typical arithmetic axioms. She found a "simple and elegant axiom system" for successor and divisibility arithmetic, with a second-order induction axiom; this theory has the same provable consequences as the usual arithmetic theory as well as her "artificial" translated system. She was unable to prove that the "simple and elegant" system with first-order induction has the same provable consequences, however, and to our knowledge this remains open.

This mention of induction turns us to a second matter concerning the topicality of proofs of IP. Our definition of a topic also included the inference rules that determine the identity of a problem or theorem. Logicians differentiate between several different versions of arithmetic induction; each of these will determine a different topic, for an investigator who accepts that version of induction. Classical first-order induction suffices for the (Robinsonian) Euclidean proof as does intuitionistic first-order induction and second-order induction; thus, the Euclidean proof is topically pure for each of these three topics. Turning to finitary arithmetic as a topic of IP, where the induction axiom is limited to primitive recursive arithmetic (following Tait 1981), the Euclidean proof can again be seen to be topically pure. This is because it inducts on no formula of arithmetic complexity higher than $\Sigma_1^0$, and $I\Sigma_1$, the arithmetic theory with induction limited to $\Sigma_1^0$, is typically thought equivalent to primitive recursive arithmetic (see Hájek and Pudlák 1998, pp. 44–47). Finally, taking feasible arithmetic as a topic of IP, matters are cloudier. On Parikh's identification of feasible arithmetic with $I\Delta_0$, where induction is limited to formulas with bounded quantifiers, it is open whether there is a topically pure proof of IP. We do know that the Euclidean proof fails in this setting, since $I\Delta_0$ does not prove that every product of primes exists (see D'Aquino 1992, p. 13).

In this example, we have seen how we need not settle on any particular topic as being the "right" one, but can instead identify many different topics, each of which license different proofs as being topically pure or impure. This is typical. As we saw earlier, Coxeter thought that distance did not belong to the topic of the Sylvester–Gallai theorem, because straight lines should be defined in terms of betweenness. By contrast, Legendre (1794) held that "the line is the shortest path from one point to another" (p. 1). This would give rise to a metrical topic for the Sylvester–Gallai theorem, on which the metrical solution by L. M. Kelly presented by Coxeter would in fact be topically pure (see Coxeter 1948, p. 28; also Arana and Mancosu 2012, section 4.6).

The question of what exactly is contained in a problem's topic is difficult. We can see some of this difficulty in Alexander Paseau's study of proofs of the compactness theorem in mathematical logic (see Paseau (2010); also see section 2 of Arana 2009). The compactness theorem for first-order logic says that if every finite subset of a set of first-order sentences has a model, then the set itself has a model. Students of logic learn Leon Henkin's proof of this result, one step of which hinges on adding elements to the model being constructed that "witness" the truth of existential sentences in this model. Paseau asks whether Henkin's use of witness completion is intrinsic to compactness. One could argue "that the notion of a witness is intrinsic to understanding the existential quantifier, part of the language of which the first-order compactness theorem is about" or that "witness-completeness is intrinsically connected to the concepts in the statement of compactness, because the latter says that some set of sentences has a model, and to exhibit a model one needs to be able to refer to its elements" (p. 77). It is not clear, however, on what terms such arguments are to be made. Paseau concludes that "the extent to which a proof uses notions foreign to the theorem it proves can be unclear, even indeterminate, so that questions of intrinsicness can be correspondingly difficult to answer or unanswerable."

Indeed, one might resist the notion of topic, that there is anything definite that is "suggested by the content of the theorem." Penelope Maddy (2000) derides Solomon Feferman's interest in "teasing out 'what is implicit in the concepts and principles' in a given theory" (p. 417, quoting Feferman 1998, p. 122), as well as what is "part of the very concept of set," as "philosophical niceties." Instead, she argues that we should take what she calls a "naturalistic point of view" in making sense of mathematical practices, drawing instead on "specifically mathematical considerations, considerations directly linked to the goals of the particular practice in question" (p. 415). In fact, our discussion of topics here does exactly that. Topical purity is one goal, among others, of particular mathematical practices, and we can observe how the actors of these practices make judgments about what is and is not topically pure by how they carry out their purity-seeking practices. From this we can see how the actors "tease out" the topics of their problems.

We can attempt to get a foothold on these worries by turning to a plausibly topically *impure* proof of IP, Hillel Furstenberg's topological proof. The proof (presented and discussed in some detail in Detlefsen and Arana 2011, §§4–5) proceeds by putting a topology on the integers with arithmetic progressions as the basic open sets. After showing that these open sets are in fact also closed, one supposes that there are finitely many primes, looking for a contradiction. The union of all sets of products of primes is then a finite union of closed sets and thus closed, and contains all integers except $\pm 1$. Then $\{-1, 1\}$, as the complement of a closed set, is open, a contradiction since the basic open sets are all infinite. This proof is topically impure for any investigator for whom commitments about topological notions like open set and basis set do not play a role in determining the content of IP.

In response, one might observe that Furstenberg's proof employs only point-set topology, formulable in a weak subsystem of set theory. Reinhard Kahle and Gabriele Pulcini have highlighted Idris Mercer's recasting of Furstenberg's proof into a proof where "no topology on $\mathbb{Z}$ ever comes into play" and in which its topological notions are "replaced by easy results involving the basic set-theoretic operations of union and intersection" (see Mercer 2009; and Kahle and Pulcini 2018, p. 132). Kahle and Pulcini conclude that Furstenberg's proof is only a case of "apparent impurity," whose "resort to such extraneous notions is nothing else but an avoidable roundabout." They judge set theory, at least this basic part, to belong to IP's topic, and thus hold that Mercer's proof is topically pure.

By adding set theory to the topic of an arithmetic theorem, Kahle and Pulcini are in sync with what we may call "set-theoretic descent": that all mathematics, deep down, is about sets. For IP, one might think that a result about the natural numbers is really a result about the *set* of natural numbers; or that mathematical induction is a rule of inference only for inductively defined sets. More generally, one might hold that set theory is the "basis" of mathematics, in that the content of every mathematical problem or theorem is fully determined by its set-theoretic articulation. As John Burgess (2022) puts it:

> Set theory provides a framework for the rigorous development of all mathematics. Each branch, group theory or field theory or whatever, is concerned with some special kind of set-theoretic structure, groups or fields or whatever, and the "axioms" of the theory are merely the definition of the class of structures in question. (p. 28)

On this view, all of mathematics is "about" sets, no matter how things may appear, and so naturally set theory will belong to every problem's topic.

This kind of view, that formulations of ordinary mathematics occlude its real content, is not exclusive to set-theoretic descent. Let us return to Fermat's Last Theorem. Briefly, a nontrivial integral solution to the equation of Fermat's Last Theorem that is greater than 2 can be understood as giving rise to an elliptic curve, whose "modularity" – "a kind of two-dimensional generalization of the familiar sine and cosine functions from trigonometry" (see Harris 2019) – is established by a result known as the modularity theorem (formerly known as the Shimura–Taniyama–Weil conjecture). Before Wiles, number theorists knew that the elliptic curve in question, if modular, would have certain properties that it in fact does not have. Wiles and Richard Taylor were able to prove the modularity theorem in the case needed for Fermat. Thus no nontrivial integral solution greater than 2 to the equation of Fermat's Last Theorem is possible. Writing about the modularity theorem, the number theorist Barry Mazur (1991) observes:

> One of the mysteries of the Shimura-Taniyama-Weil conjecture, and its constellation of equivalent paraphrases, is that although it is undeniably a conjecture "about arithmetic," it can be phrased variously, so that: in one of its guises, one thinks of it as being also deeply "about" integral transforms in the theory of one complex variable; in another as being also "about" geometry. (p. 596)

Mazur asserts that the modularity theorem is doubtlessly an arithmetic proposition, but one that can be reformulated in other terms, involving quite different parts of mathematics.

Mazur's recognition that theorems admit multiple comprehensions lets us accommodate the urge behind set-theoretic descent and other views about the clash between "face value" and what we might call "deeper" contents. We need not concede that the deeper content is the "truer" content, what a problem or theorem is "really" about. Instead, we can simply conclude that different topics for whatever problem is in question have been found: a basic topic, composed of what determines the problem's content taken at face value, and a deep topic, including the set theory that can be used to define this content. Indeed, there might be many different levels of set-theoretic analysis that can define this content, some of which use intermediate definitions like that of union or intersection, as in Mercer's set-theoretic reformulation of Furstenberg's proof, others using fewer and fewer auxiliary definitions in favor of just the primitive notions of set and membership. These different degrees of what we might call "analytic depth" will determine different topics. Rather than the exclusivist view that one of the deeper topics is the "right" one for every investigator, that an investigator who does not pursue a higher degree of analytic depth has misunderstood her own problem, we want to keep a place for the investigator who wants to solve a problem with means limited to its basic topic.

We might wonder if the urge to identify the "true" content of problems or theorems with deep contents are driven by inferentialism, the view that contents are determined by their roles within inferential practices. If one identifies the content of a mathematical claim in terms of its inferential connections, then one is forced to identify the content of a mathematical claim with what we have called the "deep" content. However, if a mathematical claim has only this deep content, then, as we will argue, there is no way to make sense of the importance of topical purity in mathematical practice. Given that we must make sense of the importance of topical purity in mathematical practice if we are to take that practice seriously, we must reject inferentialism about content.

We begin this argument by looking at how some philosophers have taken contents to be deep contents. Daniel Isaacson has argued that some sentences that appear to be purely arithmetic on face value in fact have hidden or tacit "higher-order," i.e. infinitary, nonarithmetical content. Gödel sentences and the Paris–Harrington sentence are arithmetically equivalent to sentences expressing metamathematical properties of arithmetic by means of Gödel coding (see Paris and Harrington 1977). Moreover, these sentences are

> shown to be true by an argument in terms of truths concerning some higher-order notion, and in each case also a converse holds, so that the only way in which the arithmetical statement can be established is by an argument which establishes the higher-order truth. The relationship of coding constitutes a rigid link between the arithmetical and the higher-order truths, which pulls the ostensibly arithmetical truth up into the higher-order. (Isaacson 1996, pp. 220–221)

As a result, Isaacson maintains that "the understanding of these sentences rests crucially on understanding this coding and our grasp of the situation being coded" (p. 214). The key is the provable equivalence between the Gödel sentences and the coded metamathematical statements, since this shows that these sentences all have the same inferential role in whatever theory their equivalence can be demonstrated. (John Baldwin has added that this can be treated model-theoretically by replacing the notion of inferential role of a given statement with the collection of its models: see Baldwin 2018, p. 33, chapter 12.)

Michael Hallett has echoed Isaacson's argument for a different theorem, the planar Desargues theorem. This theorem says that if two triangles lying in the same plane are such that the lines connecting their corresponding vertices intersect at a point, then the intersections of their corresponding sides are collinear (see Figure 4). As documented at length in Arana and Mancosu (2012), a projective proof of this planar result was known in solid (that is, three-dimensional) geometry since Desargues, by proving a solid version of Desargues' theorem and then projecting that result into the plane, but no purely planar proof had been found by the end of the nineteenth century. As we chronicled in Arana and Mancosu (2012), the search for a purely planar and projective proof of this result occupied many, including Karl Georg Christian von Staudt, Felix Klein, Giuseppe Peano, and David Hilbert. It also gave rise to a fascinating

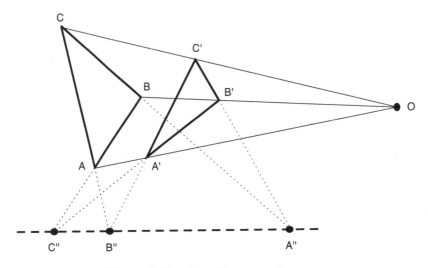

**Figure 4** The planar Desargues theorem.

pedagogical debate in Italy about whether planar and solid geometry should be taught together – "fusionism" – or separately. Hilbert clarified the matter in the last years of the nineteenth century, bringing the methods developed for proving the independence of the parallel postulate from the other Euclidean axioms to bear on planar Desargues. This work was the context for his remarks on topical purity that we quoted earlier in this section. We will narrate this work now in order to give and respond to Hallett's argument.

Say that a plane is Desarguesian if it satisfies the planar Desargues theorem. Hilbert showed that if a planar geometry satisfies the planar incidence axioms, the order axioms, and the parallel axiom, in his axiomatization of geometry, then that plane is not necessarily Desarguesian. But if all the axioms of incidence are used, not only the planar axioms but also the spatial axioms (like that there are at least four points not lying in the same plane), then that plane is necessarily Desarguesian. Hence planar Desargues is a necessary condition for a plane's being an element of a spatial geometry; or to put it another way, for a plane's being "embeddable" into space. Hilbert also showed that planar Desargues is a sufficient condition for a plane's being embeddable into space. That is, he showed that a plane satisfying the planar incidence axioms, with order and parallels, and also satisfying planar Desargues, will also satisfy the spatial incidence axioms. Hilbert proved this by showing firstly, given a planar geometry satisfying the planar incidence, order, and parallel axioms, how to construct its "algebra of segments," and that if this plane satisfies planar Desargues, multiplication in this algebra is associative, so that this algebra is an ordered division ring. Thus, if a plane is Desarguesian, then that plane is "coordinatized" by a division ring. He secondly showed how this ordered division ring can be used to construct a model of the spatial incidence, order, and parallel axioms, that is, a model of spatial geometry. (In fact, order is inessential for these results.) As a consequence, Hilbert (2004) said, "[planar] Desargues is a necessary condition for the plane's being regarded as a plane in space ... the only thing that distinguishes the plane from space, and we could say that everything that can be proven in space can now be proven with Desargues in the plane" (p. 240). That is, Desargues' theorem can be used as a replacement for Hilbert's spatial axioms; it has the same provable consequences as those axioms in Hilbert's axiomatic system. Or, to put it another way, a plane's being Desarguesian is a necessary and sufficient condition for that plane's being embeddable in a spatial geometry.

While spatial considerations would seem "at first sight" to be impure for proving Desargues' theorem, Hallett (2008) infers from Hilbert's work that they are not, for Desargues' theorem is in fact a theorem with spatial content, albeit hidden or tacit spatial content. As he puts it:

> What this shows is that that [sic] the Planar Desargues's Theorem is a *sufficient* condition for the orderly incidence of lines and planes, in the sense that it can be used to *generate* a space. We thus have an explanation for why the Planar Desargues's Theorem cannot be proved from planar axioms alone: the Planar Desargues's Theorem appears to have spatial content. (p. 229)

In contrast to Hilbert's view that "the content of Desargues' theorem belongs completely to planar geometry," Hallett maintains that Hilbert's work shows that planar Desargues has spatial content. From this, Hallett (2008) concludes:

> The examples we have considered show that often we have to adopt a *non-elementary* point of view in order to achieve results about apparently elementary theorems. ... [T]hey also show that apparently elementary propositions contain within themselves non-elementary consequences, often in a coded form. (p. 249)

Hallett does not further explain his theory of tacit content, but in a footnote to this last sentence he notes that "[t]here is surely here more than an analogy with the 'hidden higher-order content' stressed by Isaacson in connection with the Gödel incompleteness phenomena for arithmetic," citing Isaacson's paper.

Isaacson holds that Gödel sentences have higher-order content, despite being expressed in purely arithmetical terms, in virtue of having the same inferential role as sentences expressed in higher-order terms. Hallett takes the same position with Desargues' theorem, replacing "higher-order" with "spatial." They both echo Carnap (1937) in *Logical Syntax of Language*, who wrote, "[t]he question whether two *sentences* have the same *logical* sense is concerned only with the agreement of the two sentences in all their consequence-relations" (p. 42). Carnap contrasts this "logical" construal of meaning with "psychological" construals of meaning for which the "images" associated with a sentence are determinative. On our reading, Isaacson and Hallett are adopting Carnap's notion of logical content as the "hidden" content of the theorems they are studying. As Hallett (2008) puts it, "Hilbert's axiomatic method abandons the direct concern with the kind of knowledge the individual propositions represent because they are about the primitives they are, and concentrates instead on what he calls 'the logical relationships' between the propositions in a theory" (p. 212). Thus Hallett sees Hilbert's "organizational" practice as yielding a way to determine the content of theorems of axiomatic geometry: their content is determined by their inferential role within axiomatic theories. He reads Hilbert's results as showing that planar Desargues plays the inferential role of a spatial sentence, and concludes that it has (tacit) spatial content. As a result, the classical spatial proof of planar Desargues draws only on what is "suggested by the content of the theorem." and is thus topically pure, in Hallett's judgment. A similar conclusion could be drawn for Gödel sentences and the Paris–Harrington statement (though Isaacson does not do so).

In response, we again invoke the distinction between basic and deep topics. These equivalencies that we have been discussing do not force this distinction to collapse. If the content of the planar Desargues theorem were spatial, even if only tacitly, it would seem to follow that an investigator with no beliefs or commitments concerning space (such as a character of Edwin Abbott's (1884) novel *Flatland*) could not understand Desargues' theorem. But this is implausible, since Desargues configurations are purely planar phenomena, and thus the sort of thing that Flatlanders normally understand. This is why efforts to conflate basic and deep content fail: they take the results of lengthy enquiries for starting points. The mathematician who said that Fermat's Last Theorem is really about elliptical modular functions did not mean that a student encountering number theory for the first time must first master complex analysis and algebraic geometry before trying to understand a problem about Diophantine equations. Rather, knowledge of this identification is the result of years of effort.

Furthermore, slippage from basic to deep topics threatens to obliterate topical purity as a genuine constraint. Indeed, Hallett says as much in his introduction to Hilbert's 1898–1899 lectures, declaring that Hilbert's work "reveals that Desargues' *planar* Theorem has hidden *spatial* content, perhaps showing that the spatial proof of the Planar Theorem does not violate 'Reinheit' after all" (see Hilbert 2004, p. 197). If we were to replace basic topics with deeper ones systematically in this manner, seeing that topical purity is in these cases assured, then the continuing importance of purity as an epistemic objective would cease to be intelligible. That would be a significant loss on our part as philosophers of mathematics; it would be to withdraw our claim to make sense of the practice we purport to study in order to promote the philosophical agenda of inferential role semantics for mathematics.

None of that is to say that deep topics are not topics, or that theorems cannot have hidden or tacit content. Rather, it is to say that basic topics make sense of the commitments that must be engaged by an investigator to work with a problem, to begin an inquiry with it, but not necessarily the commitments that will allow her to understand the problem fully. What those commitments are can only be found a posteriori, by means of investigation into problems.

Our point of view is that each problem can have many topics, and some can generally be said to be more basic or deeper than others. There is, as far as we can see, no precise way to measure this kind of depth (though we will address one such candidate, reverse mathematics, in our discussion of elemental purity later). The question is then, which topic should be used to evaluate topical purity claims? Our methodology is that this is a question of philosophical modeling. We can consider particular purity attributions and try to identify the topic or topics that best match the actors' practices. This is what we have tried to do here in our examples. For instance, it would be hard to understand why someone who accepted a spatial topic for planar Desargues would have struggled so much with the question of whether topical purity is possible in that case. We should then resist the claim that the best topic to study in making sense of purity attributions about planar Desargues is a solid one. We can then study what makes topical purity valuable in a more general way, treating the topic of a problem as a parameter. Then any solution determined to be topically pure for a given topic can be said to apport this particular value. This will be our approach in Section 4.4.

All this being said, there has been some work in recent years trying to show how the topics of problems can be more precisely determined. As we discussed earlier, Baldwin has taken a model-theoretic approach to topics, as the collection of models of a statement. Kahle and Pulcini (2018) say that the topic of a problem should include not only the objects that the problem is about, but also the objects contained in the closure of the operations occurring in that problem (p. 134). They call this collection of objects the "ontology" of the problem, the smallest numerical domain closed under its operations, and similarly define the ontology of a proof. Robin Martinot (2023) follows Kahle and Pulcini in focusing on the objects that proofs and theorems are about, calling her precisification of topical purity, "ontological purity." Like Baldwin, and Kahle and Pulcini, she reads the ontology off the vocabulary and axioms of the statements and proofs in question.

Kahle and Pulcini call a proof "operationally pure" if the ontology of the proof is a subset of the ontology of the problem. For example, the operational closure of addition and multiplication is the set of natural numbers; adding the operations of subtraction and division, the operational closure becomes the rational numbers. An operationally pure proof of IP can draw on the rationals, then, even if the theorem ranges only over the natural numbers. In general, topics construed operationally are more inclusive, with regard to objects, than our basic topics.

These "ontological' readings of topical purity are ways to try to make more precise what are the topics of problems. As the authors acknowledge, they are set-theoretically dependent ways of doing so, and this will distort topics in ways we have already explained. It is unsurprising that Mercer's recasting of Furstenberg's proof of IP is pure on Kahle and Pulcini's account, for they have built the closures of union and intersection into IP's topic. Their topics are accordingly deeper than our basic ones in general.

## 3.3 Syntactic Purity

Another way to clarify purity is to treat it syntactically. In this section we will discuss one attempt to do so, emerging from proof theory (and discussed more fully in Arana 2009).

The setting is Gerhard Gentzen's sequent calculus formulation of the first-order predicate calculus without equality, where each step of a proof consists of sequents $A_1, \ldots, A_m \vdash B_1, \ldots, B_n$ where the $A_i$ and $B_j$ are formulas. Proofs in sequent calculus have axioms of the form $A \vdash A$. The inference rules consist of logical rules, the introduction and elimination rules for logical constants, plus a few structural rules, mostly for switching formulas around. One structural rule needs singling out, the "cut" rule, which has the form

$$\frac{\Gamma \Rightarrow \Delta, A \qquad A, \Gamma \Rightarrow \Delta}{\Gamma \Rightarrow \Delta},$$

where $A$ is called the "cut formula." Cuts are commonly compared to lemmas in informal proofs. To prove $\Gamma \vdash \Delta$ (say, concerning circles and lines), a cut uses something about $\Gamma$, $\Delta$, and something new, represented by $A$ (say, concerning right angles). More precisely, just as a lemma may draw on resources that are not used elsewhere in the proof, in a cut inference the cut formula occurs in the upper sequent but not in the lower sequent and hence is not a "subformula" of the conclusion: the subformulas of a given statement are all the substrings of the formulas comprising that statement that are themselves formulas.

In this framework we can measure the distance between a theorem and a proof by the number of formulas in a proof that are not subformulas of the theorem. When this number is zero, we may call this proof *Gentzenian pure*, and have in any case a measure of the degree of impurity of the proof, in this syntactic sense. This purity measure is appealing because it is sharply determinate when a proof is pure; indeed, it is decidable in the sense of the theory of computation.

Gentzen's interest in what we are calling Gentzenian purity was related to his mathematical work. Gentzen showed that in the sequent calculus, every proof of a statement can be transformed into a cut-free proof of that statement. This result, known as cut-elimination, implies that every provable statement in the sequent calculus has a proof such that all of the proof's formulas are subformulas of the statement proved. Gentzen (1934–1935) described the importance of this *subformula property* as follows:

> The final result is, as it were, gradually built up from its constituent elements. The proof represented by the derivation is not roundabout in that it contains only concepts which recur in the final result ... No concepts enter into the proof other than those contained in its final result, and their use was therefore essential to the achievement of that result. (pp. 88, 69.)

In Gentzen's sequent calculus, every provable statement has a Gentzenian pure proof. As the proof theorist Gaisi Takeuti (1987) added, "This means that any theorem in the predicate calculus can be proved without detours, so to speak" (pp. 21–22).

Being syntactic, this measure is sensitive to formulations. Consider again the infinitude of primes (IP), that for all natural numbers $a$, there exists a natural number $b > a$ such that $b$ is prime. This result can be formulated in the language of first-order Peano arithmetic:

$$\forall a \exists b [b > a \wedge \forall x [\exists y (x \cdot y = b) \to (x = 1 \vee x = b)]]. \tag{3.1}$$

The familiar Euclidean solution can be formulated straightforwardly in the language of first-order Peano arithmetic, but a sticking point, as we have seen already for its informal analogue, will be its use of the successor function. No such function symbol occurs in (3.1), and so no formula involving the successor function is a subformula of (3.1). Thus a formalization of the Euclidean proof that uses successor will be Gentzenian impure. We have already seen that the Euclidean proof is geographically pure and that the Robinsonian reformulation of this proof using successor is topically pure. Gentzenian purity thus differs from the other purity measures we have considered.

Another limitation of Gentzenian purity concerns its scope. Gentzen and Takeuti's enthusiasm stemmed from the fact that every provable statement in their formal systems has a Gentzenian pure proof, since cut-elimination implies the subformula property. But as Jean-Yves Girard (1987) has observed, "The cut-elimination theorem holds for predicate calculus, but fails for first-order theories, as soon as they contain proper axioms" (p. 104). By "proper axioms" Girard means nonlogical axioms like $\Rightarrow A \to B$ and $\Rightarrow A$ , rather than the axioms of the form $A \vdash A$ of Gentzen's sequent calculus. He shows that there is no cut-free proof of $\Rightarrow B$ from $\Rightarrow A \to B$ and $\Rightarrow A$ in sequent calculus, by checking every way of proving $\Rightarrow B$ from these axioms. As a result, there is no Gentzenian pure proof of $\Rightarrow B$ from $\Rightarrow A \to B$ and $\Rightarrow A$.

In general, then, the guarantee of Gentzenian purity assured for purely logical systems does not hold for systems with mathematical axioms. Sara Negri and John von Plato (2001) have attempted to overcome this limitation by developing a means of adding nonlogical axioms to sequent calculi while preserving a subformula property (in chapter 6). Their strategy is to add axioms not as initial sequents of proofs, but rather as new inference rules, in such a way that cut-elimination is more or less preserved. They give a general strategy for converting axioms into inference rules and prove that every (classical) quantifier-free theory can be converted to such an extension of sequent calculus, where the theory's axioms have been replaced with inference rules following this general schema. Using this strategy, they obtain inference rule extensions of sequent calculus for the first-order predicate calculus with equality, partial orders, and plane affine geometry, among others. They next prove a cut-elimination theorem for such axiomatic extensions of sequent calculus and obtain a version of the subformula property for these extensions. They show that all the formulas occurring in proofs in the resulting systems are either subformulas of the conclusion, or atomic formulas.

This might be thought to salvage something like Gentzen's observation for sequent calculi with nonlogical axioms and thus to provide for a syntactic measure of purity. However, Negri and von Plato's methods at present only apply to quantifier-free theories, and there is reason to think these methods cannot be extended to all nonlogical theories. That is not to say that this strategy cannot be carried out further or that other syntactic measures of purity cannot be developed. But we have seen how purity is frequently construed in terms of content, as in Hilbert.

## 3.4 Logical Purity

At the start of this section we saw Dieudonné characterize purity as a search for economy of means, means that are maximally "close" to what is being proved. We observed that this characterization can be untangled into one sense of purity in which means of proof of a theorem are close to that theorem if they are contained in the theorem or to the branch of mathematics to which it belongs. This was the goal of our discussions of geographical, topical, and syntactic purity. Dieudonné's characterization can also be read as saying the means of proof are close to the theorem if they are no stronger than what is being proved. We now want to show how purity in this sense functions.

How we should understand "stronger" here is a chief concern. One such sense has been evoked by Anand Pillay (2021), in a discussion of pure proofs of the Sylvester–Gallai theorem:

> There is a context consisting of points and lines in $\mathbb{R}^2$ and a statement about such points and lines. What do we have to know (in terms of assumptions) about this context to prove the statement, and is there a minimum natural collection of such assumptions, or axioms, (other than the statement itself) needed? Of course, some properties of the basic notions of points and lines (and incidence) will be needed, but maybe not everything about the real field $\mathbb{R}$. (p. 196)

Purity in this sense limits a proof to what is logically necessary for proving it.

In Arana (2008) we tried to make this purity constraint more precise, and John Baldwin (2018) later improved upon our formulation (pp. 267–268). He calls a collection of assumptions $S$ "fully logically minimal" for a statement $P$ if there is a proof of $P$ from $S$ and there is no set of assumptions $S'$ such that there are proofs of all the elements of $S'$ from $S$ and a proof of $P$ from $S'$, but no proof of the elements of $S$ from $S'$. He then defines a proof of a statement $P$ as *logically pure* if it draws only on assumptions from a collection of assumptions that are fully logically minimal for $P$. While this shows one way how talk of logical minimality can be made precise, Baldwin observes that his notion of logical purity is a stronger version of the notion we called "strong logical purity" in Arana (2008): a proof of a statement $P$ from a set of assumptions $S$, with background assumptions $T$ that we call a "base theory," is strongly logically pure over $T$ if there is a proof of (the elements of) $S$ using $P$ and (the elements of) $T$ as assumptions. That is, over the base theory $T$, $P$ and $S$ are logically equivalent.

Baldwin then observes that "strong logical purity has a long history including Sierpinski's equivalents of the continuum hypothesis in the 1920s, Rubin's 101 equivalents of the axiom of choice," as well as Victor Pambuccian's "reverse geometry" (Pambuccian 2001, p. 393; Pambuccian 2005, p. 19) and Harvey Friedman and Stephen Simpson's "reverse mathematics" (on which more soon; see Friedman 1976, Friedman 1975, and Simpson 2009). "These are," Baldwin says, "searches for the weakest hypotheses in terms of proof theoretic strength"

(p. 268). Similarly, Dieudonné's view of purity as the search for proofs no stronger than what is being proved can thus be seen as an instance of logical purity.

## 3.5 Elemental Purity

There is another reading of strength of means of proof giving rise to a related but distinct purity measure. When Coxeter (1989) decries Kelly's solution to the Sylvester–Gallai as impure, he adds that "it is like using a sledge hammer to crack an almond" (p. 181). Strength here is not merely logical strength. What it might be can be gleaned by reflecting on number theorists' use of the term "elementary."

The term "elementary" in number theory goes back at least to Edmund Landau. In his textbook on prime number theory, Landau (1909) says he will show how far one can get in proving the prime number theorem by "elementary methods" [*elementaren Methoden*], by which he means, in addition to ordinary arithmetic considerations, some real analytic means, namely finite sums and properties of the logarithm, but must avoid the integral calculus and complex analysis (p. viii). As already noted, this quest for an "elementary" proof of the prime number theorem is widely acknowledged to have ended in success with proofs by Atle Selberg and Paul Erdős (Selberg 1949 and Erdős 1949). Selberg (1949) characterized his proof as "elementary" because "it uses practically no analysis, except the simplest properties of the logarithm" (p. 305). This usage has now solidified in number-theoretic practice, so that in contemporary number-theoretic textbooks like Nathanson (2000), elementary proofs are defined as those that "do not use contour integrals, Cauchy's theorem, or other results from analytic function theory, but only basic facts about arithmetic functions and the distribution of prime numbers" provable by the means Landau and Selberg singled out (p. 280).

What is elementary about these proofs? A senior number theorist told me, in a personal communication, that an elementary proof is one that does not use analytic continuation or the Fourier inversion theorem, which are considered "mysterious" and "deep" results of complex analysis. Elementary proofs may use other less "deep" properties of analytic functions, however. This epistemic reading of elementarity dates at least to Landau (1909), who stressed that problems concerning the distribution of primes, including the prime number theorem, are "also understandable by the layman" [*auch dem Laien verständlich*] (p. v).

Here, though, there is ambiguity. Some proofs are hard to follow, on account of their intricacy or length, although using concepts that are easy to understand, while others are easy to follow although using concepts that are difficult to understand. Harold Diamond (1982) shows how this distinction colors the language used to evaluate such proofs:

> The approach to the prime number problem proposed by Riemann, using a function of a complex variable generated by arithmetic data, came to be called *analytic*. On the other hand, direct real variable treatment of arithmetic data, such as the method of Chebyshev, came to be called *elementary*. We shall follow this usage here. To avoid confusion, we shall (with apologies to Sherlock Holmes) use the word *simple* for "easy to understand." It will be seen that some elementary arguments are far from simple. (p. 554)

On this view, a proof is not elementary on account of its length or its surveyability (compare Floyd 2021, section 4.4). Rather, its elementarity is a function of the difficulty of the components of the proof to comprehend.

Difficulty to comprend is a matter for the cognitive science of mathematics (see Gilmore, Göbel, and Inglis 2018), but its research focuses on rudimentary mathematics rather than the sort that occupies us here. We could instead focus on interpretability strength, a perspective that emerged from work in computability theory, proof theory, and descriptive set theory (see Dean and Walsh 2017). As a most basic level we can follow Hilbert's (1931) attention to finitary reasoning, "the fundamental way of thinking that I hold as necessary for mathematics and in general for all scientific thought, understanding and communication, and without which mental activity is not at all possible" (p. 486). There is a connection here with "elementary" signifying what is understandable by the layman as in Landau. Bill Tait (1981) called this "a minimal kind of reasoning presupposed by all non-trivial mathematical reasoning about numbers" (p. 525) and identified the formal theory PRA (for primitive recursive arithmetic) as formalizing this body of reasoning. To this theory, we can add more axioms and arrive at proof-theoretically stronger systems, as is done in reverse mathematics. Stephen Simpson has observed that the "Big Five" theories studied by reverse mathematics correspond to well-established epistemic foundational programs in the philosophy of mathematics: for instance, that $RCA_0$ corresponds to the constructivism of Errett Bishop Bishop (1967), and $ACA_0$ to the predicativism of Weyl (1918) and Feferman (2005) (see Eastaugh 2019 for a discussion of these correspondences). Thus we have a series of formal theories graded by their interpretability strength, and a story about how these degrees of strength can be assessed epistemically.

Reverse mathematics seeks to answer what Simpson (2009) calls the "Main Question": "which set existence axioms are needed to prove the theorems of ordinary, non-set-theoretic mathematics?" (p. 2). It works by identifying proving logical equivalences between theorems and antecedently interesting set-theoretic theories like the aforementioned Big Five, over a logically weaker base theory. Put thusly, reverse mathematics is a search for strongly logically pure proofs. But it is more than that. The epistemic calibration by interpretability strength mentioned earlier means that reverse mathematics identifies the epistemically weakest assumptions capable of proving given results. It does this by identifying what Denis Hirschfeldt calls the "combinatorial core," and what Benoît Monin and Ludovic Patey call the "computational content," of mathematical theorems (Hirschfeldt 2014, p. 2; Monin and Patey 2022, p. 475).

So far we have looked at elementarity measured epistemically or cognitively, that can be measured comprehensionally as with Landau and the number theorists, or computationally as in reverse mathematics. Another way to measure elementarity, which we can call "ontic," would order statements in terms of some objective order of priority. Such a measure is characteristic of classical rationalist views held for instance by Aristotle, Leibniz, Bolzano, and Frege, as we saw in Section 2, on which it is held that there is an objective hierarchy of truths whose recapitulation and exhibition by "scientific demonstrations" or "groundings" provide for understanding of the truth in question (see Detlefsen 1988). There is a wide-ranging literature on grounding today (see Correia and Schnieder 2012), and the notion has been applied by contemporary philosophers of mathematics, sometimes in the context of purity (see Lange 2019 and Poggiolesi and Genco 2023).

We can now bring all this together to define another sense of purity. We say that a proof of a theorem that only draws on what is more elementary than the theorem is *elementally pure*. Having distinguished two measures of elementarity, we can distinguish two notions of elemental purity. In the first sense, an elementally pure proof of a theorem would involve only assumptions that are cognitively prior to the theorem. We can understand or grasp the proof before understanding or grasping the theorem. Dieudonné's characterization of purity as a search for economy of means is of this type. So is Hilbert's consistency program, as Kreisel (1969) suggested: "Hilbert's idea was very much the same as the widely current idea that an arithmetic theorem must have an arithmetic proof, or even that a 'simple' statement, if it can be proved at all, must have a simple proof. ... *the autonomy of elementary mathematics*" (p. 60).

In the second sense, an elementally pure proof would involve only assumptions that are metaphysically prior to the theorem. That is, in the order of being (if not our understanding), the proof proceeds from the more basic to the less basic. This second kind of elemental purity can be seen in Bolzano and Frege, for example, in Section 2.

## 4 Values of Purity

In his biographical memoir on Kurt Gödel, Kreisel (1980) wrote the following about purity:

> The *logical* question is to settle to what extent purity of methods can be achieved – in all of mathematics, parts of mathematics, in fact, in logic or metamathematics itself. But this leaves open the *philosophical* question whether purity of methods is at all basic, in the sense of fundamental, to mathematical knowledge, the sort of thing one cannot know too much about. (p. 167)

In this section we want to address this question, what is the *value* of purity for mathematical knowledge.

## 4.1 Purity and Rigor

Kreisel continues:

> But also there is the void created by simply not saying out loud what (knowledge) is gained by impure proofs, for example by analytic proofs in number theory: knowledge of *relations between the natural numbers and the complex plane* or, more fully, between arithmetic and geometric properties....if this conflicts with some ideal of rigour, so much the worse for the ideal (which is being tested). (p. 167)

In addition to raising the parallel question of the value of *impurity*, which we will address alongside the value of purity, Kreisel describes purity as an "ideal of rigour." A rigorous proof can be characterized as a proof free of errors or one with no gaps (compare Stanley Tanswell 2024, p. 5; Hamami 2014, p. 9). On this view, an impure "proof" would not be a proof at all. In Section 2 we saw Aristotle say that "we cannot, for instance, prove geometrical truths by arithmetic." We also saw Scaliger's Aristotelian critique of Archimedes' solution to the quadrature problem by exhaustion as "worthless," as summarized by van Roomen. Such Aristotelian views hinge on the necessity of purity for demonstrations capable of providing the best kind of knowledge, *epistēmē*. Impure proofs can play a different, inferior epistemic role, giving what Aristotle called in *Posterior Analytics* A13 "knowledge of the fact" rather than "knowledge of the reason why," justifying belief in the conclusion without revealing the reason why the conclusion necessarily holds (see Allen (2001) for a discussion of what Aristotle calls "inferences from signs").

Elemental purity in particular has been lauded for its contribution to rigor. A chief reason we seek proofs is to obtain conviction in their conclusions. A proof whose concepts are more mysterious than those of the conclusion, or whose steps are less evident than the conclusion, will be deficient in providing such conviction. This is the context in which we should consider Ingham's remarks concerning a "Tauberian" theorem of G. H. Hardy and J. E. Littlewood proved in Hardy and Littlewood (1919): "This theorem and its relation to the theory of numbers were first investigated by Hardy and Littlewood, but their proof does not provide a proof of the prime number theorem, since it depends explicitly on a theorem a little deeper than the prime number theorem itself" (compare Ingham 1932, p. 39). *Does not provide a proof* of the prime number theorem: Ingham suggests that an elementally impure proof fails in one key task of a proof, namely in providing conviction of its conclusion, on account of what Ingham judges to be a kind of circularity. Evidently there is an elementary "proof" of the prime number theorem from Hardy and Littlewood's theorem, but since the proof of Hardy and Littlewood's theorem draws on "deeper" (on our reading, harder to comprehend and hence less evident) means than the prime number theorem, this elementary "proof" fails to be a proof at all. Whatever doubt one has in the prime number theorem, this alleged proof does not provide sufficient evidence for assuaging that doubt. In this regard, an elementally impure proof is circular. It instead enmeshes its reader in further mystery. Elemental purity thus has the epistemic virtue of avoiding this kind of circularity and thus contributing toward conviction in the statement proved.

## 4.2 Purity, Understanding and Explanation

We now turn away from rigor and toward proofs giving the reason why. In Section 3 we saw Dieudonné promote purity on the basis that "one must always try to *understand* what one is doing as well as one can." Understanding and explanation are commonly linked by philosophers of mathematics, with explanatory proofs yielding understanding (see Tappenden 2005). As we discussed in Section 3.5, philosophers have recently linked mathematical explanations and proofs that "ground" their conclusions. Such work naturally turns to Bolzano, whose interest in purity we discussed in Section 3 in the context of his project of organizing domains of mathematical knowledge (see Rusnock 2022).

Several recent works, however, have shown how purity and explanation come apart (see McCarthy 2021, Pincock 2023, pp. 37–38). We can focus, for instance, on Mark Steiner's account of explanation, and give examples of proofs that are pure but not explanatory, and explanatory but impure. Steiner argues that inductive proofs that the sum $S(n)$ of the first $n$ positive integers equals $\frac{n(n+1)}{2}$ are not explanatory, but a similar kind of analysis to the one in Section 3.2 for the infinitude of primes gives that bounded inductive proofs are topically pure (see Arana 2023, section 4). Marc Lange (2019) gives other such examples with proofs by "brute force" that he argues can be pure but generally not explanatory (section 2). Next, Steiner (1978) argues that complex-analytic proofs of theorems about real-valued functions can be explanatory, but these will generally not be (topically) pure (pp. 18–19).

Indeed, Patrick Ryan (2021) has argued that impurity, rather than purity, makes for better explanations in mathematics. He argues that Hillel Furstenberg's topically impure ergodic proof of Szemerédi's theorem in additive combinatorics is explanatory by revealing "the dichotomy between structure and randomness" at the heart of the result (p. 34). Endre Szemerédi's original, purely combinatorial proof, by contrast, seems to be topically impure but, according to Ryan, not explanatory (also see Arana 2015, pp. 168–170, for a discussion of purity in the context of Szemerédi's theorem). Ryan appeals to the "simplicity and unification" afforded by Furstenberg's proof and thus aligns himself with the unification model of mathematical explanation exemplified by Philip Kitcher's work (see Kitcher 1981 and Kitcher 1989). Similarly, Ellen Lehet (2021) has argued that impurity can promote explanation, on account of the "generality and unification that accompany these impure methods" (p. 79). Ryan and Lehet thus echo Suzanne Bachelard (1967), who acknowledged purity as a regulative principle in contemporary mathematics, but maintained that a too strict preference for purity over impurity would sterilize the development of a unified mathematics (p. 32).

Lehet's praise for the generality of impure proofs in contemporary mathematics, particularly by means of category-theoretic proofs, should be put into perspective. A topically pure proof will use only those resources required for understanding the content of the theorem, and will thus draw on a minimum of epistemic resources. A logically pure proof uses the logically weakest hypotheses possible for its conclusion. These proofs will accordingly have wide range, capable of application to a variety of settings with stronger hypotheses. The case that impurity better provides for generality than purity is thus equivocal.

That pure proofs draw on minimal resources ensures other benefits. Topically pure solutions to problems require minimal epistemic resources for their comprehension and transmission. Since such solutions draw only on those definitions, axioms, and inference rules that determine the content of the problem, an agent who understands a problem has understood everything necessary to understand and communicate a topically pure solution of it. Elementally pure proofs minimize comprehensional resources in a different way, in that they require nothing more difficult to comprehend than what is needed to comprehend the conclusion. Recall Kreisel's characterization of Hilbert's program, quoted at the start of Section 2, that "finitist theorems should have finitist proofs." Since finitary proofs were taken by the Hilbert school to be more secure than infinitary proofs, the minimization of comprehensional resources in finitism illustrates the value of elemental purity (as would a related point about predicativist proofs of predicative theorems).

The geometer Corrado Segre (1891) wrote that in addition to the scientific value of this minimality afforded by purity, it has "didactic" value (pp. 396–397). Augustus De Morgan (1849) observed similarly that the mixing of geometry and algebra poses difficulties for students. As he wrote:

> Those who introduce *algebraical* symbols into elementary geometry, destroy the peculiar character of the latter to every student who has any mechanical associations connected with those symbols; that is, to every student who has previously used them in ordinary algebra. Geometrical reasoning, and arithmetical process, have each its own office: to mix the two in elementary instruction, is injurious to the proper acquisition of both. (p. 92)

To these pedagogical accounts of the value of purity, we can add Dieudonné's remark, in the now oft-mentioned quote at the start of Section 3, that purity is "good discipline for the mind". In Detlefsen and Arana (2011, pp. 5–6), we called this an "intervenient" value of purity, in that it contributes to the training of the capacity to reason rather than to the distinctively epistemic value of purity.

## 4.3 Geographical Purity and Local Knowledge

Until now we have said nothing specifically about the value of geographical purity. Detlefsen (1990a) has written about Poincaré's concern for "subject-specific insight...the easy, loping stride of one familiar with the twists and turns of a given local terrain" (pp. 502–503). Taking a branch of mathematics as a "local terrain," geographical purity is thus a kind of localism about mathematical knowledge, whose value we will now investigate.

Penelope Maddy (2001) described this localism as follows:

> Mathematicians in fields other than set theory often feel that set theoretic thinking doesn't capture the special sensibility that is essential to their subject, that it doesn't capture the way an algebraist, a topologist, or a geometer thinks. This seems quite true. Set theory is an individual branch of mathematics in its own right, with distinctive approaches and insights and methods of its own, approaches, insights and methods often quite different from those of algebra, topology or geometry. (p. 18)

She stresses the locality of knowledge within particular branches, noting that branches come with their own ways of thinking and working. Rather than thinking of branches as divided by subject matters – algebra by groups, rings,

modules, and fields; geometry by manifolds; set theory by sets – she says that
the essence of each branch consists in the "special sensitivity" practitioners of
that branch will come to acquire.

Gaston Bachelard (1966) drew attention to such localisms with his notion
of "regional rationalisms," organizations of particular scientific practices.
Bachelard calls such regional developments "cultures" that are socially determined by the fact of internal consensus about the rational values within each
culture's practices, about what that scientific culture's goals are and how best
they can be accomplished (p. 133). He focuses on the regionality of cultures
of physics, leaving such a discussion for mathematics for a time when more
mathematicians are occupied with its foundations (p. 119) – a project that his
daughter, Suzanne Bachelard (1967), would begin in her study of purity and
impurity in representations of imaginary numbers by algebraic, geometrical,
and topological considerations.

Karine Chemla and Evelyn Fox Keller have brought renewed attention
to the notion of cultures in scientific practices, including mathematics, in
their book Chemla and Keller (2017). Adopting the term "epistemic cultures,"
from Karin Knorr Cetina's work (see Knorr Cetina 1999) and from Keller's
own earlier work, they identify antecedent work in that of Gilles-Gaston
Granger (1968), Alistair Crombie (1994) and Ian Hacking (1992) on styles of
scientific thought and practice (compare Mancosu (2021) and Rabouin (2017)
for recent work on mathematical styles). Chemla and Keller, even in the title of
their book, *Cultures Without Culturalism*, warn against cultural essentialisms,
such as identifying epistemic cultures with national or ethnic identities, as in
Orientalist explanations of Japanese science (see Ito 2017), or the Nazi Ludwig
Bieberbach's identification of different mathematical "styles" as racially determined (see Segal 2003, pp. 361–368; we noted the practical consequences of
this latter identification in Section 1). Instead, an epistemic culture is, like for
Bachelard, a particular way of knowing and working.

We have spoken of "ways of knowing." This matter deserves a full treatment
of its own, but we can give at least a hint of what we mean. Mathematicians frequently observe that different parts of mathematics support different
ways of thinking. Timothy Gowers (2008a) has observed, for instance, that
"there is a definite difference between algebraic and geometric methods of
thinking – one more symbolic and one more pictorial – and this can have
a profound influence on the subjects that mathematicians choose to pursue"
(p. 2). While this sort of thinking was widespread into the nineteenth century, and reinforced by Kant's dichotomy of the forms of intuition, it was then
tainted by its associations with the scientific racism of the Nazis (as discussed
in the introduction). More recently this type of view has been cast in cognitive

terms (see Lakoff and Núñez 2000). The significance of this for the unity of mathematics has been noted by A. R. D. Mathias (1992), speculating "that the physiological separation by the brain of the processing of spatial from the processing temporal thought supports the thesis that a complete unification of mathematics is not possible" (p. 11).

Mathematicians commonly formulate projects in ways coherent with there being different mathematical cultures: algebraic and geometric cultures, for instance. Consider firstly Colin Rourke and Dennis Sullivan's article, Rourke and Sullivan (1971). They describe their purpose as finding a "geometrical definition" of the Kervaire obstruction, a notion in topology, and state their workings at a couple of points as finding a "more geometrical proof" of particular statements. Secondly, consider Stéphane Sabourau's article, Sabourau (2010), in differential geometry. Responding to earlier work by Florent Balacheff, Sabourau aims "to present an alternative (more geometrical) proof of the local extremality of the Calabi-Croke sphere, which does not rely on the uniformization theorem" of Poincaré (p. 549). We could similarly give examples of mathematicians seeking more algebraic proofs, more arithmetical proofs, more topological proofs, more combinatorial proofs, and so on. The point is that the disciplines of mathematics pertinent to geographical purity are understood by many practitioners as cultures in the sense of Chemla and Keller. Geographical purity is a localism, a preference for what is local to a particular mathematical culture in proving results deemed to belong to that culture. A mathematician might hold that a geometric approach to a result affords different knowledge than an algebraic approach, and so favor a geometric proof of a geometric theorem for the particular kind of knowledge that proof promises.

## 4.4 Topical Purity and the Stability of Knowledge

We turn now to an epistemic value of topical purity, one we have called in Detlefsen and Arana (2011) the *stability* account. In brief, we have argued that pure proofs provide for enduring, *stable* knowledge of their conclusions. In the following we will synthesize and amplify this view.

We have seen that the partisans of deep content often change the theorems being proved. One seeks to prove a theorem about parabolas, for instance, but after having grasped its connections with algebra, one arrives instead at a theorem about equations – a theorem with a good solution, perhaps, susceptible to being generalized to other cases. All the same, we may have reasons to prefer the *original* theorem and desire a solution to *it*. This is to take a *vectorial* conception of problem solving, wherein our investigations are directed toward a particular problem. On this conception, a solution is a solution to a particular problem to the extent that it is directed at *that* problem and not some other. A solution may succeed as a solution to some different problem while failing as a solution to the problem toward which it was directed.

Problem solving (of which theorem proving is a chief means) aims to relieve the "specific" ignorance represented by that problem. On this view, a problem is an irritation, to be removed by solving the problem. By calling problem-solving a "relief," we stress the connection between the search for knowledge and the satisfaction of desire that Aristotle identified in writing that all men by nature desire to know. Just as the satisfaction of a desire is a relief, so is the resolution of a problem.

Every solution to a problem, pure or impure, provides such relief. But how *stable* is this relief? To describe stability as we understand it, we draw on the following observation of Plato (1997b), from the *Meno*:

> To acquire an untied work of Daedalus is not worth much, like acquiring a runaway slave, for it does not remain, but it is worth much if tied down, for his works are very beautiful. What am I thinking of when I say this? True opinions. For true opinions, as long as they remain, are a fine thing and all they do is good, but they are not willing to remain long, and they escape from a man's mind, so that they are not worth much until one ties them down by (giving) an account of the reason why....After they are tied down, in the first place they become knowledge, and then they remain in place. (97e-98a, p. 895)

In Plato's metaphor, the difference between mere true opinion and knowledge is that true opinion is transient while knowledge perdures. I cannot know a proposition while also believing that at some time in the future that that proposition will be false or no longer justified. Similarly, to believe that a solution solves a problem, I must also believe that it will continue to be a solution in the future. We call this epistemic state *stability* and hold that the knowledge engendered by a solution is best when it is stable. Solutions should thus be stable with respect to changes in our epistemic position; they should perdure as solutions as long as the problem being solved perdures. We will make the case that topically pure solutions engender knowledge that is more stable than the knowledge engendered by topically impure solutions in general, and thus better realize this ideal of knowledge.

The key to our case is the observation that there are two different ways to solve a problem. Firstly, we may provide an answer to that problem. Secondly, we may rationally *dissolve* that problem. This second type of solution arises from inspection of the etymology of the verb "to solve," from the Latin *solvere*: to loosen, release, unbind. Both types of solutions eliminate the specific ignorance represented by a problem, either by providing the desired knowledge, or by eliminating that ignorance as a source of desire for knowledge. When the ignorance represented by a problem has been eliminated for an agent, by some rational means, then that problem ceases to be a problem for her and thus has been solved.

We have spoken of rational means of dissolving problems. More precisely, we say that a problem has been *dissolved* when, on account of a change in the investigator's beliefs or attitudes concerning the problem's content, that problem no longer represents an ignorance for that investigator. For instance, if I rescind my commitment that every natural number has a successor, then I will no longer understand the natural numbers as a discrete sequence, and thus I will have dissolved (for me) basic arithmetic problems like the infinitude of primes. Then those problems are no longer problems for me, in that they no longer represent specific ignorances that I seek to relieve. When I dissolve a problem in this fashion, then, I have solved that problem in our second sense. By contrast, if I rescind my belief that every holomorphic function is analytic, my understanding of the infinitude of primes does not change, and so the problem is not dissolved.

We may now relink this discussion with the notion of a problem's topic. Any rescission of an element of a problem's topic dissolves that problem for that investigator, and hence that problem is no longer an ignorance for that investigator. This is the case even though a different problem may have been opened by this rescission, maybe even a better problem by some measures; but the *original* problem has been closed by being dissolved.

To explain how topically pure solutions more stably solve the problems toward which they are directed, we need to discuss the rescission of solutions. An investigator rescinds a solution to a problem when that investigator no longer accepts one of the premises or inferences of that solution, and what remains of that solution no longer determines the propositional content of that problem. A recent example of rescission comes from symplectic geometry, where Dusa McDuff and Katrin Wehrheim brought attention to errors in work by Kenji Fukaya (see Hartnett 2017). In order to solve the Arnold conjecture, a key problem in symplectic geometry about a kind of fixed point of symplectic manifolds, Fukaya and his collaborator Kaoru Ono introduced the notion of Kuranishi structures in Fukaya and Ono (1999). Their work on this notion, however, was not sufficiently intelligible to the community working in symplectic geometry to be widely accepted. In 2012 McDuff and Wehrheim made public errors they had found in Fukaya and Ono's work and began publishing work that fixed the errors they had found (see McDuff and Wehrheim 2015). These errors were not unique to Fukaya; indeed, Wehrheim pointed out that some of McDuff's own work contained errors as well, rooted in unclarity in the foundations of symplectic geometry as developed until then. While Fukaya did not think that McDuff and Wehrheim's work contributed any new ideas, calling them a "mere technicality," the community acknowledged that their work was necessary to make precise what Fukaya had not. As a result, Fukaya's methods, suitably corrected, have been accepted by the symplectic geometry community, though new methods for the problems arising from the Arnold conjecture have also been developed.

In this episode we can see several moments of acceptance and rescission by different communities. At first, imprecise ideas about symplectic manifolds seem to have been widely accepted by symplectic geometers at large. Fukaya and Ono's work advanced new ideas, but their imprecision blocked their wider acceptance. McDuff and Wehrheim's "whistleblowing" (adopting their term) made a part of the community rescind their acceptance of many of the methods they had earlier taken up, though Fukaya did not do so. After McDuff and Wehrheim's work, the wider community accepted the modified Fukaya methods. We thus see how the messiness of mathematical practice can involve rescission, change, and acceptance of modified methods, though we make no claims about the purity of any of this work. (Thanks to Moon Duchin for bringing this example to my attention.)

With the notion of solution rescission clarified, we may return to the question of how topically pure solutions more stably solve the problems toward which they are directed than topical impure solutions. This is because rescission of a topically pure solution by an investigator will generally dissolve that problem for that investigator. Since each premise and inference of a topically pure solution belongs to the problem's topic, their rescission will dissolve that problem. That is not necessarily so for topically impure proofs.

We have identified stability as an *ideal* of knowledge: knowledge that perdures through changes in our epistemic situation – an *invariance* condition on knowledge. As we have seen, the knowledge of a theorem engendered by a topically pure proof of that theorem perdures through changes in our epistemic attitude toward that theorem, but that is not necessarily so for topically impure proofs. Thus, other things being equal, topically pure proofs are better at providing stable knowledge of their conclusions than are topically impure proofs.

## 4.5 The Simplicity of Purity and Impurity

Impurity, like purity, is valued by many mathematicians, as we have noted throughout this work. Douglas Marshall has shown how thinking about impurity, which he calls "internal applications of mathematics," contributes to work on traditional questions in metaphysics and philosophy of science (cf. Marshall 2023). We have been taking the view that purity and impurity can coexist as values, since we can give multiple proofs of theorems. But whatever advantages pure proof may have over impure proof would be countered by disadvantages if impure proof were *systematically* simpler than pure proof. We will now address this possibility.

Such claims are common in the literature. Carlo Cellucci (1985) has claimed that "the use of 'impure' methods leads to a marked improvement in efficiency" (p. 173). In Section 2 we saw Lagrange's call for the unity of algebra and geometry on efficiency grounds. Jacques Hadamard (1945) famously observed that "the shortest and best way between two truths of the real domain often passes through the imaginary one" (p. 123).

We can distinguish two different questions concerning the simplicity of pure and impure proof. Firstly, we can investigate whether impure proofs are generally simpler to *verify* than pure proofs of the same statement; that is, to check the validity of a given proof candidate (see Detlefsen 1990b, p. 376f24; also Detlefsen 1996, p. 87). Secondly, we can investigate whether impure proofs are generally simpler to *discover* than pure proofs of the same statement.

Both questions can be approached by proof theory, though there is a considerable literature pointing out the limitations of proof theory for philosophical reflection on proofs in informal mathematical practice. In Arana and Stafford (2023), section 5, we both discuss this literature and defend the significance of proof theory for such questions. Briefly, at whatever level of granularity we consider a proof, it will have some logical structure, and proof theory can be applied to this structure. This is so even if there are other epistemic features of proof to which proof theory cannot be made sensitive.

In Arana (2017) we addressed the first question, whether impure proofs are generally simpler to verify than pure proofs of the same statement. In this work we considered conservative extensions of the formal theory Primitive Recursive Arithmetic (PRA) mentioned in Section 3.5, in which proofs of theorems of PRA can be given that are, arguably, impure. Specifically, we looked at *arithmetic* extensions adding induction schemas for more inclusive classes of arithmetical formulas, and *set-theoretic* extensions adding comprehension principles for certain kinds of sets. The former make for cases of elemental impurity, while the latter make for cases of topical impurity. To compare the simplicity of proofs of theorems of PRA with proofs of these same theorems in extensions of PRA, we consider the "speed-up" of proofs in extensions of PRA. We say that theory $T_1$ is at most a polynomial speed-up of $T_2 \subset T_1$ when for every $\varphi$ provable in $T_2$, the length of the shortest proof (measured in terms of total number of symbol occurrences) of $\varphi$ in $T_2$ is less than some fixed polynomial multiple of the length of the shortest proof of $\varphi$ in $T_1$. Next, $T_1$ is said to have a roughly superexponential speedup over $T_2 \subset T_1$ when for every $\varphi$ provable in $T_2$, the length of the shortest proof in $T_2$ of $\varphi$ is a superexponential multiple of the length of the shortest proof of $\varphi$ in $T_1$. Superexponential speedups are considered to be significant, while polynomial speedups are not (following the tradition in complexity theory; see Dean 2016, §2.2). Using this notion of speedups, we showed that there is no evidence of a general pattern of improvement in simplicity in moving from pure to impure proof, thus answering the first question negatively.

In Arana and Stafford (2023) we addressed the second question, whether impure proofs are generally simpler to discover than pure proofs of the same statement. We discussed Alessandra Carbone's *topological* measure of proof simplicity, building on work of Richard Statman, for proofs in propositional sequent calculus with rules permitting inferences with computations of binary functions (see Carbone 2009; Statman 1974). Associating each proof with a graph, this measure evaluates the simplicity of discovering a proof by the topological genus of its associated graph. Carbone's idea is that topological genus is a measure of "discovermental complexity" because it is a measure of what Statman calls the "global structural complexity" of a proof, since genus is a property of a graph as a whole; and a high global structural complexity means that the proof has many highly interconnected ideas of which the discoverer or reader must keep track. Intuitively, then, the higher the genus of a proof, the more difficult it is to discover that proof, on account of its convolutedness.

Recalling the identification of pure proofs with cut-free proofs that we saw in Section 3.3, Carbone proves that there are pure (that is, cut-free) proofs of arbitrarily high genus. This can be taken to say that pure proofs may have arbitrarily high "discovermental complexity." Since no such result is known for impure proofs, one can conclude that impure proofs may not have arbitrarily high discovermental complexity, and thus, that impure proofs are generally simpler to discover than pure proofs.

We nevertheless have good reasons to reject this conclusion. Firstly, it is possible that Carbone's main result is also obtainable for proofs with cut. In that case, the epistemic asymmetry between pure and impure proofs would be broken. Secondly, her present result applies only to propositional sequent calculus, but an adequate formalization of ordinary mathematics would need more expressive and inferential resources, including quantifiers and the ability to begin proofs with nonlogical axioms. As we saw in Section 3.3, extending the result to these wider contexts is likely to be difficult. Thirdly, the proofs with large genus that Carbone builds have graphs with many edges, and this is what makes them hard to comprehend. But this complexity is not a special feature of proofs with high genus. It will also be true of many fully formalized proofs (in PA, say) that are not typically judged to be particularly complex. Informal proofs that "correspond" to these formal proofs suppress a lot of the intermediate logical steps that are generating complexity here, suggesting that this complexity may be in part an artifact of formalization. Fourthly, Carbone's measure assigns a special kind of graph to proofs, what Sam Buss (1991) calls a "logical flow graph". But, we can argue, the genus of the logical flow graph of a proof does not capture the global structural complexity of that proof, because it ignores the structure introduced by the logical connectives, by definition. Instead, the logical flow graph tracks where a formula is within the sequents of a proof, its "flow" through the proof. But the application of logical rules have structural effects on proofs. For instance, right $\wedge$ binds together two proofs, one for each conjunct, but this structure is entirely missing from logical flow graphs. Thus Carbone's genus measure misses structural features of proofs that should be tracked by a discovermental simplicity measure.

For both of the two questions about the relative simplicity of pure and impure proofs, then, the evidence from proof theory is not definitive. That should not mean that we dismiss the evocations of the efficiency of impure proof that we have seen from Lagrange, Hadamard, and Cellucci. It is to say that attempts to make their claims precise, by the best formal means we have today, are not successful.

# 5 Conclusions

In the last section, we saw Kreisel question whether purity is "at all basic, in the sense of fundamental, to mathematical knowledge, the sort of thing one cannot know too much about." We have tried in this Element to show that it is. Purity has been an ideal of mathematical proof since antiquity and remains so today. As we have seen, the study of purity brings in questions of mathematical practice, metaphysics, epistemology, semantics, methodology, and logic, as well as psychology, pedagogy, sociology, and politics. We have distinguished several different types of purity, and we have explored what is valuable about these types of purity.

Let us recapitulate the types of purity we have canvassed. We began with three types of purity concerned with measuring the proximity of proof to theorem in terms of the containment of that proof's means in the theorem or to the branch of mathematics to which it belongs. Firstly, a proof of a statement is *geographically pure* if it draws only on what belongs to the branch of mathematics to which the statement belongs. Secondly, a proof is *topically pure* if it draws only on what belongs to the content of the theorem it is proving, that is, on what must be grasped and accepted in order to comprehend that theorem. Thirdly, a proof of a statement is *Gentzenian pure* if it consists only of subformulas of that statement.

We then turned to two types of purity concerned with measuring the closeness of means of proof to theorem in terms of whether these means are stronger or not than what is being proved. Firstly, a proof of a statement is *logically pure* if it draws only on what is logically necessary for proving it. Secondly, a proof of a statement that only draws on what is more elementary than the statement is *elementally pure*. We discussed two ways to construe elementarity: as an epistemic notion that can be measured comprehensionally or computationally, and as an ontic notion in terms of some objective order of priority.

Next, we will briefly discuss some important open problems about purity. We have seen how the question of what belongs to the content of mathematical statements is difficult to determine. The topic of a problem is the family of commitments that together determine the content of that problem for a given investigator. Settling what is the topic of a problem thus rests on settling what is its content. We have distinguished basic content from deep content, in order to avoid an inferentialism about content that trivializes topical purity, but that distinction requires further clarity. We do not want to defend a "psychological" view of content in terms of "images," to use Carnap's terminology. An alternative could be a fine-grained sort of truth condition that could be something like a Fregean sense. When we consider the claims that "all triangles have three sides" and "all triangles have interior angles summing to 180 degrees," we see that someone can grasp the content of both claims, be sure that the first one is true, and yet doubt that the second one is true. By this Fregean argument, we could conclude that they have different basic contents. This, at any rate, is an idea to be developed.

Turning to a second open problem, we have seen how purity can be framed as a preference for the local. A next stage of this work would be to investigate further the interplay between this localism and the enduring importance of reciprocity between mathematical subject matters. We have begun this with our notion of deep content, but there is much more to do. One approach is by means of the notion of *translation*. Logic gives us tools to model translatability with the notion of *interpretation*. We say that a theory $T$ is interpretable in another theory $T^*$ if there is a way of translating the primitives of $T$ into formulas of $T^*$ such that the induced map $\varphi \mapsto \varphi^*$ is such that if $T$ proves $\varphi$, then $T^*$ proves $\varphi^*$. Two theories are mutually interpretable if each interprets the other. A canonical example of interpretability is the representation of non-Euclidean plane geometries in Euclidean space developed in the nineteenth century. Mathematicians chose a way to translate "point" and "line" in a nonstandard fashion within

Euclidean space so as to validate the non-Euclidean axioms. Other examples are the interpretability of the axioms of groups in the axioms of fields, and of the Peano axioms in Zermelo–Fraenkel set theory.

The connection between purity and interpretability has been started in Arana (2017), Baldwin (2018), and Martinot (2023). But we must be careful about the limits of this approach. Hilbert showed that the division ring axioms are mutually interpretable (with parameters) with the axioms for Desarguesian projective planes. If interpretations preserve content, then Hilbert's result shows that statements concerning Desarguesian projective planes have the same meaning as their translations concerning division rings. Thus purely geometric talk of projective planes and purely algebraic talk of division rings has the same meaning. This goes against five hundred years of thinking in mathematics, where algebraic thinking and geometric thinking have been thought to be distinct, engendering different types of understanding.

Another approach, which may eventually lead to new formal notions of interpretability, comes from reflecting further on translatability. Poincaré (1891) described how we can think about the relation between Euclidean and non-Euclidean geometries in terms of translatability:

> Let us construct a kind of dictionary by making a double series of terms written in two columns, each corresponding to each, in the same way that in ordinary dictionaries the words of two languages that have the same meaning correspond to each other. Let us then take the theorems of Lobachevsky and translate them with the help of this dictionary like we translate a German text with the help of a German-French dictionary. *We will thus obtain the theorems of ordinary geometry.* (p. 771)

This metaphor of a "dictionary" has been adopted by algebraic geometers. As just one example, Karen Smith and her coauthors describe Hilbert's Nullstellensatz in such terms: "This famous theorem is the first entry in a dictionary that will help us translate statements about geometry into the language of algebra" (see Smith, Kahanpää, Kekäläinen, and Traves 2000, p. 19).

The dictionary metaphor is helpful because it suggests another approach to translatability and purity. No dictionary can fully capture the meanings of language. In Cassin (2004) and, ironically, in its English translation Cassin (2014), Barbara Cassin and her team have drawn attention to the limits of translation, noting in particular the difficulty of translating philosophical terms between different European languages. A member of the team of English translators of this work, Emily Apter, has shown how this difficulty holds more generally for literary translation, and how it is situated within the social and political context of globalism today (see Apter 2013). She advocates, alongside Cassin, for a pluralism of understanding of literatures, rather than a single "world" literature whose differences are erased by translation.

Mathematicians, too, have sensed this possibility. In Section 4.3 we quoted part of such a remark by Timothy Gowers (2008b), and here give the rest of it:

> It is often possible to translate a piece of mathematics from algebra into geometry or vice versa. Nevertheless, there is a definite difference between algebraic and geometric *methods of thinking*—one more symbolic and one more pictorial—and this can have a profound influence on the subjects that mathematicians choose to pursue. (p. 2)

In correspondence with his sister Simone, André Weil too developed such a view by way of the metaphor of the Rosetta Stone. He writes of the liaisons between number theory and geometry, in particular between algebraic number fields and the field of algebraic functions of a complex variable, brought to prominence by Dedekind and Weber in their work on the Riemann–Roch theorem. Weil stresses that these different "languages" can be translated to one another, though only partially; filling in these partial translation tables constitutes an important mathematical task for Weil. Doing so permits us to learn "the art of passing from one to the other, and to profit in the study of the first from knowledge acquired about the second, and of the extremely powerful means offered to us, in the study of the latter" (see Weil 2005, p. 340). When we encounter a difficulty in one language, we can try to translate the difficulty into one of the other languages and see if the way is clearer there. Furthermore, new results may be suggested from such translations; for instance, Alain Connes created the subject of noncommutative geometry by translating noncommutative algebra into geometry by means of the so-called "algebraic-geometric dictionary" of contemporary algebraic geometry.

The upshot of Weil's "Rosetta Stone" approach is that we may support autonomous mathematical languages and ways of working while retaining the possibility of translating to other autonomous languages. The translatability expresses the unity between these languages, while the autonomy of the individual languages expresses their disunity. This mirrors contemporary approaches to cultural pluralism, in which individual cultures and languages retain their autonomy while existing alongside other autonomous cultures and languages, all the while interacting relatively frictionlessly through translation (think, for instance, of the cultural life of Belgium or Quebec). This unity among disunity, characteristic of linguistic diversity today, is a model for the interplay of unity and disunity in mathematics. As Patrick Suppes (1978) put it:

> Personally I applaud the divergence of language in science and find in it no
> grounds for skepticism or pessimism about the continued growth of science.
> The irreducible pluralism of languages of science is as desirable a feature as
> is the irreducible plurality of political views in a democracy. (p. 6)

We advocate the same for mathematics.

We have seen in this Element another kind of pluralism, that of values. Despite the reasons we have offered to value purity, many mathematicians continue to value impurity. This does not mean that the accounts of the value of purity that we have given are wrong. Problem solving in mathematics admits considerable variety, and there are typically many solutions to each problem (Dawson 2015 and Ording 2019). Among this variety are pure and impure proofs in the various senses that we have discussed. Purity and impurity are two rational values of mathematical practice, but there are others, some of which we have already discussed, like rigor and explanatoriness. We need not think that there is just one "best" proof, because there can be many different proofs of the same theorem, each good in a different way. And of course, there can be bad proofs as well: any virtue theory must be at the same time a theory of vices.

This pluralist conception of epistemic mathematical values echoes ongoing trends in the philosophy of science, where for instance Hasok Chang (2012) has promoted what he calls "epistemic pluralism." As he puts it, "Each and every scientist is driven by a set of epistemic values simultaneously. To pretend that they are or should be devoted to the pursuit of only one epistemic value would be foolish" (p. 274). The collaborative pursuit of multiple epistemic values, such as unity and purity, contributes to a fuller understanding of mathematics. It is important to cultivate a plurality of epistemic values in order to succeed as a mathematical knower, because to know in the fullest sense requires knowing in as many different ways as we can.

# References

Abbott, E. (1884). *Flatland: A romance of many dimensions*. London: Seeley and Co.

Aigner, M., & Ziegler, G. M. (2010). *Proofs from THE BOOK* (Fourth ed.). Berlin: Springer.

Allen, J. (2001). *Inference from signs: Ancient debates about the nature of evidence*. Oxford: Oxford University Press.

Apter, E. (2013). *Against world literature: On the politics of untranslatability*. London: Verso.

Arana, A. (2007). Review of *Toward a philosophy of real mathematics*, by David Corfield. *Mathematical Intelligencer, 29*(2), 80–83.

Arana, A. (2008). Logical and semantic purity. *Protosociology, 25*, 36–48. (Reprinted in *Philosophy of mathematics: Set theory, measuring theories, and nominalism*, G. Preyer and G. Peter (Eds.), Offenbach: Ontos, 2008.)

Arana, A. (2009). On formally measuring and eliminating extraneous notions in proofs. *Philosophia Mathematica, 17*, 208–219.

Arana, A. (2014). Purity in arithmetic: Some formal and informal issues. In G. Link (Ed.), *Formalism and beyond: On the nature of mathematical discourse* (pp. 315–335). Boston: De Gruyter.

Arana, A. (2015). On the depth of Szemerédi's Theorem. *Philosophia Mathematica, 23*(2), 163–176.

Arana, A. (2017). On the alleged simplicity of impure proof. In R. Kossak & P. Ording (Eds.), *Simplicity: Ideals of practice in mathematics and the arts* (pp. 207–226). Cham: Springer.

Arana, A. (2023). Purity and explanation: Essentially linked? In C. Posy & Y. Ben-Menahem (Eds.), *Mathematical knowledge, objects and applications: Essays in memory of Mark Steiner* (pp. 25–39). Cham: Springer.

Arana, A., & Burnett, H. (2023). Mathematical hygiene. *Synthese, 202*(110), 1–28.

Arana, A., & Mancosu, P. (2012, June). On the relationship between plane and solid geometry. *Review of Symbolic Logic, 5*(2), 294–353.

Arana, A., & Stafford, W. (2023). On the difficulty of discovering mathematical proofs. *Synthese, 202*(38), 1–29.

Avigad, J. (2003). Number theory and elementary arithmetic. *Philosophia Mathematica, 11*, 257–284.

Babbitt, D., & Goodstein, J. (2011, February). Federigo Enriques's quest to prove the "Completeness Theorem." *Notices of the American Mathematical Society, 58*(2), 240–249.

Bachelard, G. (1966). *Le rationalisme appliqué* (Third ed.). Paris: Presses Universitaires de France.

Bachelard, S. (1967). *La représentation géométrique des quantités imaginaires au début du xixe siècle*. Paris: Conférences du Palais de la Découverte.

Baldwin, J. (2018). *Model theory and the philosophy of mathematical practice*. Cambridge, UK: Cambridge University Press.

Bishop, E. (1967). *Foundations of constructive analysis*. New York: McGraw-Hill.

Bolzano, B. (1999). Purely analytic proof of the theorem that between any two values which give results of opposite sign there lies at least one real root of the equation. In W. Ewald (Ed.), *From Kant to Hilbert* (Vol. 1, pp. 227–248). Oxford: Oxford University Press. (Originally published in 1817; translated by S. Russ.)

Briançon, J., & Skoda, H. (1974). Sur la clôture intégrale d'un idéal de germes de fonctions holomorphes en un point de $c^n$. *Comptes Rendus de l'Académie des Sciences, Série A, 278*, 949–951.

Brigaglia, A., & Cilberto, C. (1995). *Italian algebraic geometry between the two world wars*. Kingston: Queen's University. (Translated from Italian by Jeanne Duflot.)

Brouwer, L. E. J. (1913). Intuitionism and formalism. *Bulletin of the American Mathematical Society, 20*(2), 81–96.

Burgess, J. P. (2022). *Set theory*. Cambridge, UK: Cambridge University Press.

Buss, S. R. (1991). The undecidability of $k$-provability. *Annals of Pure and Applied Logic, 53*(1), 75–102.

Cameron, D. (1995). *Verbal hygiene*. Abingdon: Routledge.

Carbone, A. (2009). Logical structures and genus of proofs. *Annals of Pure and Applied Logic, 161*(2), 139–149.

Carnap, R. (1937). *Logical syntax of language*. London: Kegan Paul, Trench, Trubner and Co., Ltd. (Translated by Amethe Smeaton (Countess von Zeppelin).).

Cassin, B. (2004). *Vocabulaire européen des philosophies: dictionnaire des intraduisibles*. Paris: Seuil.

Cassin, B. (2014). *Dictionary of untranslatables*. Princeton: Princeton University Press.

Cegielski, P. (1984). La theorie élémentaire de la divisibilité est finiment axiomatisable. *Comptes Rendus de l'Académie des Sciences – Series I – Mathematics, 299*(9), 367–369.

Cegielski, P., Matijasevich, Y., & Richard, D. (1996, June). Definability and decidability issues in extensions of the integers with the divisibility predicate. *Journal of Symbolic Logic, 61*(2), 515–540.

Cellucci, C. (1985). Proof theory and complexity. *Synthese, 62*, 173–189.

Chang, H. (2012). *Is water $H_2O$? Evidence, realism and pluralism.* Dordrecht: Springer.

Chemla, K. (1998). Lazare Carnot et la généralité en géométrie. Variations sur le théorème dit de Menelaus. *Revue d'histoire des máthematiques, 4*, 163–190.

Chemla, K., & Keller, E. F. (Eds.). (2017). *Cultures without culturalism: The making of scientific knowledge.* Durham: Duke University Press.

Collison, M. J. (1977). The origins of the cubic and biquadratic reciprocity laws. *Archive for History of Exact Sciences, 17*(1), 63–69.

Correia, F., & Schnieder, B. (2012). *Metaphysical grounding.* Cambridge, UK: Cambridge University Press.

Coxeter, H. S. M. (1948, January). A problem of collinear points. *American Mathematical Monthly, 55*(1), 26–28.

Coxeter, H. S. M. (1989). *Introduction to geometry* (Second ed.). New York: Wiley.

Crombie, A. (1994). *Styles of scientific thinking in the European tradition.* London: Duckworth.

D'Aquino, P. (1992). Local behaviour of the Chebyshev theorem in models of $I\Delta_0$. *Journal of Symbolic Logic, 57*(1), 12–27.

Davenport, H. (2008). *The higher arithmetic* (Eighth ed.). Cambridge, UK: Cambridge University Press.

Dawson, J. W., Jr. (2006). Why do mathematicians re-prove theorems? *Philosophia Mathematica, 14*(3), 269–286.

Dawson, J. W., Jr. (2015). *Why prove it again? Alternative proofs in mathematical practice.* Heidelberg: Birkhäuser.

Dean, W. (2016). Computational complexity theory. In E. N. Zalta (Ed.), *The Stanford encyclopedia of philosophy* (Winter 2016 ed.). Metaphysics Research Lab, Stanford University. https://plato.stanford.edu/archives/win2016/entries/computational-complexity/.

Dean, W., & Walsh, S. (2017). The prehistory of the subsystems of second-order arithmetic. *Review of Symbolic Logic, 10*(2), 357–396.

Dedekind, R. (1872). Continuity and irrational numbers. In W. Ewald (Ed.), *From Kant to Hilbert* (Vol. 2, pp. 766–779). Oxford: Oxford University Press. (Translated by W. Ewald.)

Dedekind, R. (1888). *Was sind und was sollen die zahlen?* Braunschweig: Vieweg.

Dedekind, R. (1932). *Gesammelte mathematische Werke* (Vol. III; R. Fricke, E. Noether, & Ö. Ore, Eds.). Braunschweig: Vieweg.

De Morgan, A. (1849). *Trigonometry and double algebra*. London: Taylor, Walton, and Maberly.

Descartes, R. (1898). *Oeuvres* (Vol. II; C. Adam & P. Tannery, Eds.). Paris: Léopold Cerf.

Descartes, R. (1902). *Oeuvres* (Vol. VI; C. Adam & P. Tannery, Eds.). Paris: Léopold Cerf.

Detlefsen, M. (1988). Fregean hierarchies and mathematical explanation. *International Studies in the Philosophy of Science 3*(1), 97–116.

Detlefsen, M. (1990a). Brouwerian intuitionism. *Mind, 99*(396), 501–534.

Detlefsen, M. (1990b, November). On an alleged refutation of Hilbert's program using Gödel's first incompleteness theorem. *Journal of Philosophical Logic, 19*(4), 343–377.

Detlefsen, M. (1996). Philosophy of mathematics in the twentieth century. In *Philosophy of Science, Logic, and Mathematics* (Vol. 9, pp. 50–123). London and New York: Routledge. (Edited by Stuart G. Shanker)

Detlefsen, M. (2008). Purity as an ideal of proof. In P. Mancosu (Ed.), *The Philosophy of Mathematical Practice* (pp. 179–197). Oxford: Oxford University Press.

Detlefsen, M. (2010). Rigor, Re-proof and Bolzano's Critical Program. In P. E. Bour, M. Rebuschi, & L. Rollet (Eds.), *Construction. Festschrift for Gerhard Heinzmann* (pp. 171–184). London: King's College Publications.

Detlefsen, M., & Arana, A. (2011, January). Purity of methods. *Philosophers' Imprint, 11*(2), 1–20.

Diamond, H. G. (1982). Elementary methods in the study of the distribution of prime numbers. *Bulletin of the American Mathematical Society, 7*(3), 553–589.

Dieudonné, J. (1969). *Linear algebra and geometry*. Boston: Houghton Mifflin Co. (Translation of J. Dieudonné, *Algèbre linéaire et géométrie élémentaire*, Hermann, Paris, third edition, 1964.)

Diophantus. (1621). *Diophanti alexandrini arithmeticorum libri sex, et de numeris multangulis liber uns*. Paris: Sebastiani Cramoisy. (Latin edition translated from the Greek with commentaries by Claude Gaspar Bachet Sieur de Méziriac)

Dirichlet, G. L. (1856). Sur l'équation $t^2 + u^2 + v^2 + w^2 = 4m$ [Extrait d'une Lettre de M. Lejeune-Dirichlet à M. Liouville]. *Journal de mathématiques pures et appliquées, 1*, 210–214.

Eastaugh, B. (2019). Set existence principles and closure conditions: Unravelling the standard view of reverse mathematics. *Philosophia Mathematica, 27*(2), 153–176.

Eilenberg, S., & Steenrod, N. E. (1945, April). Axiomatic approach to homology theory. *Proceedings of the National Academy of Sciences of the United States of America, 31*(4), 117–120.

Eilenberg, S., & Steenrod, N. (1952). *Foundations of algebraic topology.* Princeton: Princeton University Press.

Eisenstein, G. (1847). Neue Theoreme der höheren Arithmetik. *Journal für die reine und angewandte Mathematik, 35,* 117–136.

Engel, F. (1890). *Der Geschmack in der neueren Mathematik.* Leipzig: Alfred Lorentz.

Erdős, P. (1949). On a new method in elementary number theory which leads to an elementary proof of the prime number theorem. *Proceedings of the National Academy of Sciences, USA, 35,* 374–384.

Euler, L. (1758). De numeris, qui sunt aggregata duorum quadratorum. *Novi Commentarii academiae scientiarum Petropolitanae, 4,* 3–40.

Ewald, W. (Ed.). (1999). *From Kant to Hilbert* (Vol. II). Oxford: Oxford University Press.

Farrell, J., Farrell, K., & Rodgers, T. (2016). Martin Gardner and Marilyn vos Savant: A not always easy collaboration. *Word Ways, Vol. 49*(4).

Feferman, S. (1998). *In the light of logic.* New York: Oxford University Press.

Feferman, S. (2005). Predicativity. In S. Shapiro (Ed.), *Handbook of the philosophy of mathematics and logic.* Oxford: Oxford University Press.

Fermat, P. d. (1894). *Oeuvres de Fermat. Tome 2* (P. Tannery & C. Henry, Eds.). Paris: Gauthier-Villars.

Ferraro, G., & Panza, M. (2012). Lagrange's theory of analytical functions and his ideal of purity of method. *Archive for History of Exact Sciences, 66*(2), 95–197.

Ferreirós, J., & Gray, J. J. (Eds.). (2006). *The architecture of modern mathematics.* New York: Oxford University Press.

Fisch, M. (1999). The making of Peacock's *Treatise on Algebra*: A case of creative indecision. *Archive for History of Exact Sciences, 54,* 137–179.

Floyd, J. (2021). *Wittgenstein's philosophy of mathematics.* Cambridge, UK: Cambridge University Press.

Frege, G. (1980). *The Foundations of Arithmetic.* Evanston, IL: Northwestern University Press. (Translated by J. L. Austin)

Frege, G. (1984). Formal theories of arithmetic. In B. McGuinness (Ed.), *Collected papers on mathematics, logic, and philosophy* (pp. 112–121). Oxford: Blackwell. (Translated by E.-H. W. Kluge)

Friedman, H. M. (1975). Some systems of second order arithmetic and their use. In R. D. James (Ed.), *Proceedings of the 1974 International Congress of Mathematicians* (Vol. 1, pp. 235–242). Montreal: Canadian Mathematical Congress.

Friedman, H. M. (1976, June). Systems of second order arithmetic with restricted induction. I. *Journal of Symbolic Logic, 41*(2), 557–558.

Fukaya, K., & Ono, K. (1999). Arnold conjecture and Gromov–Witten invariant. *Topology, 38*(5), 933–1048.

Gentzen, G. (1934–1935). Untersuchungen über das logische Schliessen. *Mathematische Zeitschrift, 39*, 405–431. (Translated as "Investigations into logical deduction" in *The collected papers of Gerhard Gentzen*, M. E. Szabo (Ed.), North-Holland, 1969.)

Gilmore, C., Göbel, S. M., & Inglis, M. (2018). *An introduction to mathematical cognition*. London: Routledge.

Girard, J.- Y. (1987). *Proof theory and logical complexity* (Vol. 1). Naples: Bibliopolis.

Gowers, T. (Ed.). (2008a). *The Princeton companion to mathematics*. Princeton, NJ: Princeton University Press.

Gowers, T. (2008b). What is mathematics about? In T. Gowers (Ed.), *The Princeton companion to mathematics* (pp. 1–7). Princeton, NJ: Princeton University Press.

Granger, G.- G. (1968). *Essai d'une philosophie du style*. Paris: Armand.

Gray, J. (2012). *Henri Poincare: A Scientific Biography*. Princeton, NJ: Princeton University Press.

Gray, J. (2015). *The real and the complex: A history of analysis in the 19th century*. Heidelberg: Springer.

Hacking, I. (1992). 'Style' for historians and philosophers. *Studies in History and Philosophy of Science, 23*, 1–20.

Hadamard, J. (1945). *The psychology of invention in the mathematical field*. Princeton: Princeton University Press.

Hájek, P., & Pudlák, P. (1998). *Metamathematics of first-order arithmetic*. Berlin: Springer. (Second printing)

Hallett, M. (2008). Reflections on the purity of method in Hilbert's *Grundlagen der Geometrie*. In P. Mancosu (Ed.), *The philosophy of mathematical practice* (pp. 198–255). Oxford University Press.

Hamami, Y. (2014). Mathematical rigor, proof gap and the validity of mathematical inference. *Philosophia Scientiæ, 18*(1), 7–26.

Hardy, G. H., & Littlewood, J. (1919). On a Tauberian theorem for Lambert's series, and some fundamental theorems in the analytic theory of numbers. *Proceedings of the London Mathematical Society, 19*(1), 21–29.

Hardy, G. H., & Wright, E. M. (1979). *An introduction to the theory of numbers* (Fifth ed.). New York: Oxford University Press.

Harris, M. (2019, June). Why the proof of Fermat's Last Theorem doesn't need to be enhanced. *Quanta Magazine*. (https://www.quantamagazine.org/why-the-proof-of-fermats-last-theorem-doesnt-need-to-be-enhanced-20190603)

Hartnett, K. (2017, February). A fight to fix geometry's foundations: When two mathematicians raised pointed questions about a classic proof that no one really understood, they ignited a years-long debate about how much could be trusted in a new kind of geometry. *Quanta Magazine*.

Hasse, H. (1930). Die moderne algebraische Methode. *Jahresbericht der Deutschen Mathematiker-Vereinigung, 39*, 22–33.

Hilbert, D. (1899). *Grundlagen der Geometrie*. Leipzig: B. G. Teubner.

Hilbert, D. (1901). Mathematische Probleme. *Archiv der Mathematik und Physik (3rd series), 1*, 44–63, 213–237. (English translation by M. W. Newson in the *Bulletin of the American Mathematical Society* 8: 437–479, 253–297, 1902.)

Hilbert, D. (1931). Die Grundlegung der elementaren Zahlenlehre. *Mathematische Annalen, 104*, 485–494.

Hilbert, D. (1971). *Foundations of Geometry*. La Salle, IL: Open Court. (English translation of *Grundlagen der Geometrie* (B. G. Teubner, Leipzig, 1899), by L. Unger)

Hilbert, D. (2004). *David Hilbert's lectures on the foundations of geometry, 1891–1902* (M. Hallett & U. Majer, Eds.). Berlin: Springer.

Hirschfeldt, D. (2014). *Slicing the truth: On the computable and reverse mathematics of combinatorial principles*. Singapore: World Scientific.

Ingham, A. (1932). *The distribution of prime numbers*. Cambridge: Cambridge University Press.

Isaacson, D. (1996). Arithmetical truth and hidden higher-order concepts. In W. Hart (Ed.), *The philosophy of mathematics* (pp. 203–224). New York: Oxford University Press. (First published in *Logic Colloquium '85*, the Paris Logic Group (Eds.), Amsterdam, North-Holland, 1987, pp. 147–169.)

Ito, K. (2017). Cultural difference and sameness: Historiographic reflections on histories of physics in modern Japan. In K. Chemla & E. F. Keller (Eds.), *Cultures without culturalism: The making of scientific knowledge*. Durham: Duke University Press.

Jacobi, C. G. J. (1828). Note sur la décomposition d'un nombre donné en quatre quarrés. *Journal für die reine und angewandte Mathematik, 1828*(3), 191.

Jacobi, C. G. J. (1829). *Fundamenta nova theoriae functionum ellipticarum*. Regiomonti: Sumtibus Fratrum Borntraeger.

Jacobi, C. G. J. (1834). De compositione numerorum e quatuor quadratis. *Journal für die reine und angewandte Mathematik, 3*, 167–172.

Jacobi, C. G. J. (1848). Über unendliche Reihen, deren Exponenten zugleich in zwei verschiedenen quadratischen Formen enthalten sind. *Journal für die reine und angewandte Mathematik, 37*, 61–94, 221–254.

Kahle, R., & Pulcini, G. (2018). Towards an operational view of purity. In P. Arazim & T. Lávička (Eds.), *The Logica yearbook 2017* (pp. 125–138). College Publications.

Kitcher, P. (1981, December). Explanatory unification. *Philosophy of Science, 48*(4), 507–531.

Kitcher, P. (1989). Explanatory unification and the causal structure of the world. In P. Kitcher & W. Salmon (Eds.), *Scientific explanation* (pp. 410–505). Minneapolis: University of Minnesota Press.

Klein, J. (1992). *Greek mathematical thought and the origin of algebra*. New York: Dover Publications. (Translated by E. Brann)

Kleiner, I. (2012). *Excursions in the history of mathematics*. New York: Birkhäuser.

Knorr, W. R. (1978). Archimedes and the spirals. *Historia Mathematica, 5*, 43–75.

Knorr Cetina, K. (1999). *Epistemic cultures: How the sciences make knowledge*. Cambridge, MA: Harvard University Press.

Kreisel, G. (1969). Luitzen Egbertus Jan Brouwer: 1881–1966. *Biographical Memoirs of Fellows of the Royal Society, 18*, 39–68.

Kreisel, G. (1980). Kurt Gödel. *Biographical Memoirs of Fellows of the Royal Society, 26*, 149–224.

Lacroix, S.- F. (1797). *Traité du calcul différentiel et du calcul intégral* (Vol. 1). Paris: J.-B.-M. Duprat.

Lagrange, J.- L. (1772). Démonstration d'un théorème d'arithmétique. *Nouveaux Mémoires de l'Académie royale des Sciences et Belles-Lettres de Berlin, année 1770*, 123–133.

Lagrange, J.- L. (1799). Discours sur l'objet de la théorie des fonctions analytiques. *Journal de l'École Polytechnique, 2*(6), 232–235.

Lagrange, J.- L. (1876). Leçons sur mathematiques elementaires. In *Oeuvres de lagrange* (Vol. VII). Paris: Gauthier-Villars. (Edited by Joseph-Alfred Serret)

Lakoff, G., & Núñez, R. (2000). *Where mathematics comes from*. New York: Basic Books.

Landau, E. (1909). *Handbuch der Lehre von der Verteilung der Primzahlen*. Leipzig: B.G. Teubner.

Lange, M. (2019). Ground and explanation in mathematics. *Philosophers' Imprint, 19*(33), 1–18.

Legendre, A.- M. (1794). *Éléments de géométrie*. Paris: Firmin Didot.

Lehet, E. (2021, 1). Impurity in contemporary mathematics. *Notre Dame Journal of Formal Logic, 62*.

Leibniz, G. W. (1996). *New essays on human understanding*. Cambridge: Cambridge University Press. (Edited and translated by Peter Remnant and Jonathan Bennett)

Lipman, J., & Teissier, B. (1981). Pseudo-rational local rings and a theorem of Briançon-Skoda about integral closures of ideals. *Michigan Mathematical Journal, 28*, 97–116.

Lorenat, J. (2015). Figures real, imagined, and missing in Poncelet, Plücker, and Gergonne. *Historia Mathematica, 42*(2), 155–192.

Lorenat, J. (2016). Synthetic and analytic geometries in the publications of Jakob Steiner and Julius Plücker (1827–1829). *Archive for History of Exact Sciences, 70*, 413–462.

Luchins, A., & Luchins, E. (1990). The Einstein–Wertheimer correspondence on geometric proofs and mathematical puzzles. *Mathematical Intelligencer, 12*(2), 35–43.

Maddy, P. (2000). Does mathematics need new axioms? *Bulletin of Symbolic Logic, 6*(4), 413–422.

Maddy, P. (2001). Some naturalistic reflections on set theoretic method. *Topoi, 20*, 17–27.

Mancosu, P. (2021). Mathematical style. In E. N. Zalta (Ed.), *The Stanford encyclopedia of philosophy* (Winter 2021 ed.). Metaphysics Research Lab, Stanford University. https://plato.stanford.edu/archives/win2021/entries/mathematical-style/.

Marshall, D. B. (2023, 10). Internal applications and puzzles of the applicability of mathematics. *Philosophia Mathematica, 32*(1), 1–20.

Martinot, R. (2023). Ontological purity for formal proofs. *The Review of Symbolic Logic*, 1–40.

Mathias, A. (1992). The ignorance of Bourbaki. *Mathematical Intelligencer, 14*(3), 4–13.

Mazur, B. (1991). Number theory as gadfly. *American Mathematical Monthly, 98*(7), 593–610.

Mazzotti, M. (2023). *Reactionary mathematics: A genealogy of purity*. Chicago: University of Chicago Press.

McCarthy, T. (2021, 1). Induction, constructivity, and grounding. *Notre Dame Journal of Formal Logic, 62*.

McDuff, D., & Wehrheim, K. (2015). *Kuranishi atlases with trivial isotropy: The 2013 state of affairs*.

McLarty, C. (2020). The large structures of Grothendieck founded on finite-order arithmetic. *Review of Symbolic Logic, 13*(2), 296–325.

Mercer, I. (2009, April). On Furstenberg's proof of the infinitude of primes. *American Mathematical Monthly, 116*, 355–356.

Merz, J. T. (1903). On the development of mathematical thought during the nineteenth century. In *European thought in the nineteenth century* (Vol. II, pp. 627–740). Edinburgh: William Blackwood and Sons.

Michel, N. (2020). The values of simplicity and generality in Chasles's geometrical theory of attraction. *Journal for General Philosophy of Science, 51*, 115–146.

Monin, B., & Patey, L. (2022). *Calculabilité*. Paris: Calvage et Mounet.

Nathanson, M. B. (2000). *Elementary methods in number theory*. New York: Springer.

Negri, S., & von Plato, J. (2001). *Structural proof theory*. Cambridge, UK: Cambridge University Press.

Newton, I. (1972). *The mathematical papers of Isaac Newton. Vol. V: 1683–1684* (D. Whiteside, Ed.). Cambridge, UK: Cambridge University Press.

Newton, I. (2022). *Unarranged fragments, mostly relating to the dispute with Leibniz*. Cambridge, UK: Cambridge University Library. (MS Add. 3968, ff. 594r-619v. https://www.newtonproject.ox.ac.uk/view/texts/normalized/NATP00385)

O'Hara, C., & Ward, D. (1937). *An introduction to projective geometry*. Oxford: Clarendon Press.

Ording, P. (2019). *99 variations on a proof*. Princeton, NJ: Princeton University Press.

Pambuccian, V. (2001, March). Fragments of Euclidean and hyperbolic geometry. *Scientiae Mathematicae Japonicae, 53*(2), 361–400.

Pambuccian, V. (2005). Euclidean geometry problems rephrased in terms of midpoints and point–reflections. *Elemente der Mathematik, 60*, 19–24.

Pambuccian, V. (2009). A reverse analysis of the Sylvester–Gallai theorem. *Notre Dame Journal of Formal Logic, 50*(3), 245–260.

Pambuccian, V. (2011). The axiomatics of ordered geometry I. Ordered incidence spaces. *Expositiones Mathematicae, 29*, 24–66.

Panza, M. (1997). Classical sources for the concept of analysis and synthesis. In M. Otte & M. Panza (Eds.), *Analysis and synthesis in mathematics* (pp. 365–414). Dordrecht: Kluwer Academic Publishers.

Paris, J., & Harrington, L. (1977). A mathematical incompleteness in Peano Arithmetic. In J. Barwise (Ed.), *Handbook of mathematical logic* (pp. 1133–1142). Amsterdam: North-Holland.

Paseau, A. (2010). Proofs of the compactness theorem. *History and Philosophy of Logic, 31*(1), 73–98.

Pel, B. (2023). 'A remarkable artifice': Laplace, Poisson and mathematical purity. *The Review of Symbolic Logic*, 1–37.

Picard, E., & Simart, G. (1906). *Théorie des fonctions algébriques de deux variables indépendantes* (Vol. 2). Paris: Gauthier-Villars.

Pillay, A. (2021, 1). Remarks on purity of methods. *Notre Dame Journal of Formal Logic, 62*.

Pincock, C. (2023). *Mathematics and explanation*. Cambridge, UK: Cambridge University Press.

Plato. (1997a). *Collected works*. Indianapolis: Hackett. (Edited by John M. Cooper)

Plato. (1997b). Meno. In *Plato (1997a)* (pp. 870–897). (Translated by G. M. A. Grube)

Poggiolesi, F., & Genco, F. (2023). Conceptual (and hence mathematical) explanation, conceptual grounding and proof. *Erkenntnis, 88*(4), 1481–1507. doi: 10.1007/s10670-021-00412-x

Poincaré, H. (1891). Les géométries non euclidiennes. *Revue générale des sciences pures et appliqueés, 2*, 769–774. (Reprinted as chapter 3 of *Science and Hypothesis*, Walter Scott Publishing, London, 1905, pp. 35–50.)

Poincaré, H. (1902). Sur la nature du raisonnement mathématique. In *La science et l'hypothèse*. Paris: Flammarion.

Proclus. (1992). *A commentary on the first book of Euclid's Elements*. Princeton, NJ: Princeton University Press. (Translated from Greek by Glenn R. Morrow)

Rabouin, D. (2009). *Mathesis universalis – l'idée de « mathématique universelle » d'aristote à descartes*. Paris: PUF.

Rabouin, D. (2017). Styles in mathematical practice. In K. Chemla & E. F. Keller (Eds.), *Cultures without culturalism: The making of scientific knowledge*. Durham: Duke University Press.

Robinson, J. (1949). Definability and decision problems in arithmetic. *Journal of Symbolic Logic, 14*, 98–114.

Rourke, C. P., & Sullivan, D. P. (1971). On the Kervaire obstruction. *Annals of Mathematics, 94*(3), 397–413.

Rusnock, P. (2022, 02). Grounding in Practice: Bolzano's Purely Analytic Proof in Light of the Contributions. In *Bolzano's Philosophy of Grounding: Translations and Studies*. Oxford: Oxford University Press.

Ryan, P. J. (2021). Szemerédi's theorem: An exploration of impurity, explanation, and content. *The Review of Symbolic Logic*, 1–40.

Sabourau, S. (2010). Local extremality of the Calabi–Croke sphere for the length of the shortest closed geodesic. *Journal of the London Mathematical Society, 82*(3), 549–562.

Saint-Gervais, H. P. d. (2010). *Uniformisation des surfaces riemann.* Lyon: ENS Éditions. (Translated from the French by Robert G. Burns 2016)

Saint-Gervais, H. P. d. (2016). *Uniformization of Riemann surfaces.* Zurich: European Mathematical Society. (Translated from the French by Robert G. Burns)

Salanskis, J.- M. (2008). *Philosophie des mathématiques.* Paris: Vrin.

Segal, S. (2003). *Mathematicians under the Nazis.* Princeton, NJ: Princeton University Press.

Segre, C. (1891). Su alcuni indirizzi nelle investigazioni geometriche. *Rivista di Matematica, 1,* 42–66.

Selberg, A. (1949). An elementary proof of the prime-number theorem. *Annals of Mathematics, 50,* 305–313.

Simpson, S. G. (2009). *Subsystems of second order arithmetic* (Second ed.). Cambridge, UK: Cambridge University Press.

Smith, K. E., Kahanpää, L., Kekäläinen, P., & Traves, W. (2000). *An invitation to algebraic geometry.* New York: Springer.

Stanley Tanswell, F. (2024). *Mathematical rigour and informal proof.* Cambridge, UK: Cambridge University Press.

Statman, R. (1974). Structural complexity of proofs (Unpublished doctoral dissertation). Stanford University.

Steiner, M. (1978). Mathematics, explanation, and scientific knowledge. *Nous, 12*(1), 17–28.

Steinkrüger, P. (2018). Aristotle on kind-crossing. In V. Caston (Ed.), *Oxford studies in ancient philosophy* (pp. 107–158). Oxford: Oxford University Press.

Suppes, P. (1978). The plurality of science. In *Psa: Proceedings of the biennial meeting of The Philosophy of Science Association* (Vol. 1978, pp. 3–16).

Tait, W. W. (1981). Finitism. *The Journal of Philosophy, 78*(9), 524–546.

Takeuti, G. (1987). *Proof theory* (Second ed.). Amsterdam: North-Holland.

Tappenden, J. (2005). Proof style and understanding in mathematics. I. Visualization, unification and axiom choice. In P. Mancosu, K. F. Jørgensen, & S. A. Pedersen (Eds.), *Visualization, explanation and reasoning styles in mathematics* (pp. 147–214). Dordrecht: Springer.

Tappenden, J. (2008). Mathematical concepts and definitions. In P. Mancosu (Ed.), *The philosophy of mathematical practice* (pp. 256–275). Oxford University Press.

Toffoli, S. D., & Fontanari, C. (2023). Recalcitrant disagreement in mathematics: An "endless and depressing controversy" in the history of Italian algebraic geometry. *Global Philosophy, 33*(38), 1–29.

University, C. W. R. (2013, March 4). Professor shows Fermat's Last Theorem can be proved more simply. *College of Arts and Sciences News*. (https://artsci .case.edu/news/philosophy-professor-shows-fermats-last-theorem-can-be-proved-more-simply/)

van Dalen, D. (1995). Hermann Weyl's intuitionistic mathematics. *Bulletin of Symbolic Logic*, *1*(2), 145–169.

vos Savant, M. (1993). *The world's most famous math problem*. New York: St. Martin's Press.

Weil, A. (2005). A 1940 letter of André Weil on analogy in mathematics. *Notices of the American Mathematical Society*, *52*(3), 334–341. (Translated into English by Martin H. Krieger)

Weyl, H. (1918). *Das Kontinuum. Kritische Untersuchungen über die Grundlagen der Analysis*. Leipzig: Veit.

Wussing, H. (2007). *The genesis of the abstract group concept: A contribution to the history of the origin of abstract group theory*. Mineola, NY: Dover.

# The Philosophy of Mathematics

## Penelope Rush
*University of Tasmania*

From the time Penny Rush completed her thesis in the philosophy of mathematics (2005), she has worked continuously on themes around the realism/anti-realism divide and the nature of mathematics. Her edited collection, *The Metaphysics of Logic* (Cambridge University Press, 2014), and forthcoming essay 'Metaphysical Optimism' (*Philosophy Supplement*), highlight a particular interest in the idea of reality itself and curiosity and respect as important philosophical methodologies.

## Stewart Shapiro
*The Ohio State University*

Stewart Shapiro is the O'Donnell Professor of Philosophy at The Ohio State University, a Distinguished Visiting Professor at the University of Connecticut, and a Professorial Fellow at the University of Oslo. His major works include *Foundations without Foundationalism* (1991), *Philosophy of Mathematics: Structure and Ontology* (1997), *Vagueness in Context* (2006), and *Varieties of Logic* (2014). He has taught courses in logic, philosophy of mathematics, metaphysics, epistemology, philosophy of religion, Jewish philosophy, social and political philosophy, and medical ethics.

## About the Series

This Cambridge Elements series provides an extensive overview of the philosophy of mathematics in its many and varied forms. Distinguished authors will provide an up-to-date summary of the results of current research in their fields and give their own take on what they believe are the most significant debates influencing research, drawing original conclusions.

**Cambridge Elements** ⹀

# The Philosophy of Mathematics

## Elements in the Series

Printed in the United States
by Baker & Taylor Publisher Services